the food lover's guide to canning

the food lover's guide to
Canning

CONTEMPORARY
RECIPES & TECHNIQUES

CHRIS RICH
LUCY CLARK CRAWFORD

Lark Books
Asheville, North Carolina

ART DIRECTION AND PHOTOSTYLING: **Chris Bryant**

PHOTOGRAPHY: **Evan Bracken**
(Light Reflections, Hendersonville, NC)

ASSISTANT EDITOR: **Laura Dover Doran**

EDITORIAL ASSISTANCE: **Evans Carter**

PRODUCTION ASSISTANCE: **Bobby Gold**

Library of Congress Cataloging in Publication Data

Rich, Chris, 1949–
    The food lover's guide to canning : contemporary recipes & techniques /
by Chris Rich and Lucy Clark Crawford. — 1st ed.
       p.   cm.
    Includes index.
    ISBN 1-887374-46-9
    1. Canning and preserving. I. Crawford, Lucy Clark.
TT603.R43   1997
641.4'2—dc21   97-14631
                                           CIP

10 9 8 7 6 5 4 3 2 1

First Edition

Published by Lark Books
50 College Street
Asheville, NC 28801
USA

Distributed by Random House, Inc., in the United States, Canada, the United Kingdom, Europe, and Asia

Distributed in Australia by Capricorn Link (Australia) Pty Ltd., P. O. Box 6651,
Baulkham Hills Business Centre, NSW 2153, Australia

Distributed in New Zealand by Tandem Press Ltd., 2 Rugby Rd., Birkenhead, Auckland, New Zealand

Printed in Hong Kong

ISBN 1-887374-46-9

contents

introduction

CONTEMPORARY HOME CANNERS aren't usually harried country homemakers struggling to make their garden produce feed a family over the winter. They're not all female, they no longer work in kitchens or sheds as hot as saunas, and they know better than to seal their jars of jelly with paraffin. They don't line their pantry shelves with jar after boring jar of tomatoes, green beans, and peaches, either.

Today's canners—and there are thousands of them—are men and women who prepare and process food at home because they want to—not because they have to. Corporate executives and secretaries, gardeners and gourmet chefs, retirees and young hobbyists alike, they all love fine food, and they're more than willing to spend a few hours making sure they have some favorites in stock, from mouth-watering soups and exotic Indian chutneys to traditional English marmalades and savory sauces.

Ask some home canners why they indulge in this hobby, and you're likely to hear dozens of different answers. For many canners, flavor is all important. These folks insist—and rightly so—that home-canned foods, made with loving care and fresh ingredients, taste infinitely better than the canned foods sold at grocery stores. They know that comparing a commercial jam or jelly with even the simplest home-processed version is like comparing flat ginger ale with ambrosia.

Other canners are addicted to specialty foods: the high-priced chutneys and sauces that you see on gourmet-store shelves and wish you could serve more often at home. These canners have learned that preparing and processing gourmet foods themselves is much more fun than buying them.

Some canners are especially concerned with ingredients and nutrition. They like to be aware of what they're eating. When they prepare a Creole soup or cranberry marmalade at home, they know exactly how much salt or sugar is in each jar, they know their food is additive-free, and they know it's been made with the freshest possible ingredients.

Then there are the canners who find that the home-canning process itself is actually relaxing. Yes, making a batch of home-canned food requires time and effort, but there are clear rules to follow, soothing tasks to repeat, and visible, tasty results to enjoy when you're finished. After a demanding week at a high-stress job, an afternoon spent in the kitchen can feel heavenly. The smells of simmering sauces, the meditative repetitions of slicing and dicing, the sight of cooling jars lined up neatly on folded towels can all help a work-splintered self regain its focus.

Urban canners enjoy the fact that you don't have to live in the country or devote every waking hour to a garden in order to enjoy the canning process. In fact, city-dwelling canners find that searching for excellent produce and new recipes leads them to wonderful out-of-the-way markets and restaurants.

And finally, many home canners appreciate the fact that preparing and processing a batch of food never takes longer than a day. When their busy lives leave them no time for their hobby, they don't have to face the guilt so many other crafts induce—those half-knitted sweaters and half-woven baskets that lurk in closets from coast to coast.

Lucy and I are living proof that no two home canners are alike. As a nutritionist and mother, Lucy leans more heavily than I do toward a concern for ingredients. She loves being able to serve fine-tasting food that's also healthful. As a gourmet adventurer and miser, I'm most gleeful when I'm savoring a remarkable jalapeño salsa that I didn't have to buy from a store. What the two of us share is the conviction that very few hobbies are as easy to learn, as productive, or as satisfying.

If you've inherited the old suspicion that home-canned foods are potentially dangerous to eat, let go of it. Although that fear was once well founded, over the past several decades, scientists have developed rules for home canners—rules that work when they're followed. The United States Department of Agriculture (USDA) publishes updated guidelines for home canners and local Cooperative Extension Service agents work hard to make these available to the public. *The Food Lover's Guide to Canning* adheres to every one of these guidelines.

In this book, you'll find everything you need to know in order to can food safely and effectively. First, we'll introduce you to the theories that determine safe canning practices. Then we'll help you gather together your equipment and supplies. When you're ready to start, we'll walk you, step-by-step, through practice sessions in boiling-water bath canning and pressure canning—the two (and only two) USDA approved heat-processing methods. Once you're familiar with these two methods, you'll be ready to tackle any of the more than 100 recipes in this book. Welcome to the wonderful world of canning!

CHAPTER 1 the basics

EVERY HOBBY HAS ITS RULES: Hit the ball over the net, not into it; inhale when your head is above water, not under; pull up the green things you didn't plant, not the ones you did. Home canning also has rules, but in one respect they're very different from those of other pastimes. You have to learn them before, not after, you begin! Losing a game of tennis, snorting up some of your local swimming pool, or accidentally yanking up a row of immature carrots can be frustrating. Serving up home-canned green beans that haven't been heat processed properly can be downright dangerous.

Please don't let us frighten you off before you've even started. That's certainly not our intent. You'll soon realize that the theories underlying safe home-canning practices are easy to learn, and once you've put them into practice, every stage of home canning makes perfect sense.

SAFE CANNING METHODS

The basic steps of home canning couldn't be simpler. First, you prepare the food you want to can, place it in clean canning jars, and fasten lids and screw bands onto the jars. Then you heat the jars, either in a large kettle of boiling water or in a pressure canner. This *heat processing*, as it's called, destroys microorganisms that can spoil the food and also seals the jars so that other microorganisms can't get in. As the filled jars are heated, air is forced out of them. When the filled jars cool down, the vacuum created seals the lids by sucking them down tightly against the jar rims.

Today, only two methods of processing canned foods, each used for a different type of food, are known to be acceptable and safe. One is the *boiling-water bath method*, in which jars filled with high-acid foods (you'll find out what these are in just a minute) are submerged in a large kettle of boiling water for a specific length of time, depending upon the type of food being processed. The main purpose of boiling-water bath processing is to heat high-acid canned food to 212°F or 100°C (the temperature at which water boils at sea level) and to hold that temperature long enough to destroy microorganisms.

The other heat-processing method is *pressure canning*, in which jars filled with low-acid foods are processed in a pressure canner at temperatures ranging from 240°F to 250°F (116°C to 121°C)—temperatures higher than those reached in a boiling-water bath. The pressure in a pressure canner can be adjusted; you'll learn how in chapter 5.

SAFE PROCESSING TIMES

No matter which of the two processing methods you use or what size jar you use, the food must be heated thoroughly, evenly, and for a specific amount of time. For this reason, any good canning recipe will include what's known as a *processing time*, and recipes that must be pressure canned will also include a specific pressure. Never vary these times or pressures. Bread makers can subtract a few minutes when they're baking their loaves in an oven, but home canners don't have this luxury. The times and pressures provided in tested recipes for home canning affect food safety as well as flavor, texture, and color, so never tamper with them!

Recommended processing times and pressures will vary, depending upon the size of jar you use. Because they hold less, ½-pint jars require a shorter processing time than 1-quart jars. In general, however, ½-pint and 1-pint jars require the same amount of processing time in a boiling-water bath. Quart jars and 1½-pint jars are also processed for equal lengths of time.

ACIDITY

What are high-acid and low-acid foods, and why is it important to know the difference? We'll answer these questions one at a time.

Every food has an acidity strength, which is measured on a range known as the *pH scale*. *High-acid foods* are those with a pH of 4.6 and below; *low-acid foods* are those with a pH above 4.6. Fortunately, you don't need to remember long lists of foods and their acidity strengths. All fruits (including jams and jellies) and pickled products (including relishes, sauerkraut, and chutneys) are high acid. All vegetables, meats, seafood, poultry, and mushrooms are low acid.

Pickled products, by the way, even if they contain low-acid foods, are considered to be high acid. Why? Because pickled foods always include an acidifying ingredient, typically vinegar. Green peppers, for example, are a low-acid food, but pickled green peppers are high acid.

Keep in mind that the acidity of foods can be intentionally—and unintentionally—changed. Adding too much water to a high-acid pickled food as you prepare a recipe, for example, will lower its acidity. Fruits lose their acid strength when they're allowed to overripen.

Why does food acidity matter so much in home canning? Because the acid strength of the ingredients in your recipe will determine which of the two heat-processing methods you must use in order to process the food safely. The microorganisms that thrive in high-acid foods can be deactivated or destroyed at the temperature that water reaches when it boils at sea level, so high-acid foods can be safely processed in a boiling-water bath. The microorganisms that thrive in low-acid foods, however, are more heat resistant, and higher temperatures are necessary to destroy them—temperatures that can only be reached in a pressure canner.

YOUR ENEMIES

Whenever you engage in canning, you'll share the experience with literally billions of voracious and determined competitors: enzymes, yeasts, molds, and bacteria. While no one in their right mind would open or serve jars of food as obviously spoiled as those shown on the next page, some microorganisms create invisible effects. Knowing a bit about these microscopic enemies, many of which can cause serious illness when eaten, will help you understand why using the correct heat-processing method is so important.

Enzymes

These proteins, which are present in all plant and animal matter, make it possible for plants and animals to grow and mature, but unless they're deactivated, they change the color, flavor, and texture of any fresh food as it ages. To see enzymes at work, just slice an apple and watch the flesh turn brown or leave a banana on your kitchen counter for a couple of weeks!

The heat generated in either a boiling-water bath canner or in a pressure canner deactivates enzymes completely. Of course, some enzymes will fight you before you've even had a chance to pack the food into jars; they're the ones that turn the flesh of apples and pears brown almost as soon as you've sliced them. To prevent enzymes from discoloring certain foods before you can heat process them, you'll coat these foods with an antioxidant solution right after you peel and slice them (see page 33 for details).

Combining High-Acid and Low-Acid Foods

Many of the recipes in this book call for combining low- and high-acid foods. Which of the two heat-processing methods should you use? The recipes will always let you know, but the rule of thumb is easy to remember.

Unless you're dealing with a pickled product, in which an acidifier such as vinegar makes the food combination high acid, first look through the list of ingredients for the one with the lowest acidity. Then turn to the chart on pages 123–26. Look up the low-acid ingredient in the chart and process the filled jars according to the guidelines for that single ingredient, even if there isn't very much of it in the recipe. If, for example the lowest-acid ingredients in a soup are dried beans and you plan to process the soup in quart jars, look up the processing method (pressure canning) and processing time for a quart of beans (90 minutes at 10 pounds of pressure) and process the recipe accordingly.

Jars of spoiled food don't always look as horrifying as these! You'll learn how to detect less visible signs of spoilage when you read chapter 6.

Molds and Yeasts

You've probably seen mold on food before, perhaps as a fuzzy mass on aging jam. What you may not know is that molds, which prefer high-acid foods such as fruits and pickled products, produce spores that float through the air in search of a place to start growing again. When these spores find a poorly sealed jar filled with high-acid food, they grow more mold. Fortunately, heating food-filled jars to the temperature of boiling water destroys all mold spores.

Molds aren't as safe to ingest as people once thought. As many of us were growing up, we were taught to skim molds off the surfaces of jams, jellies, and cheese, and then eat the food underneath. Think twice before you do this again! Recent research indicates that molds can contain carcinogens.

Yeasts also grow on foods. Many, such as those that turn milk into yogurt and cause fermentation in beer, aren't bad for you. The types of yeast that you'll want to prevent in canned foods are the types that cause fermentation within the jars and the types that grow as a dry film on the surface of the food. Yeasts are especially fond of high-acid foods and foods with a lot of sugar in them. Like molds, they're destroyed at the temperature of boiling water.

Bacteria

Many bacteria, including staphylococcus and salmonella, can spoil food and/or cause food poisoning, but the bacteria of most concern to you will be the spore-forming type known as *clostridium botulinum*. Yes, these are the bacteria that can cause the sometimes lethal form of poisoning known as botulism. Their spores can live for many years in soil and water and are much more common than you might imagine on the surface of fresh food.

Frightened? Don't be. Botulinum on fresh food won't hurt you. These bacteria don't like high-acid foods, either, so you won't find them in correctly processed, home-canned fruits or pickled products. That's one of the reasons it's safe to process high-acid foods in a boiling-water bath.

Botulinum bacteria do love low-acid foods, however—all vegetables, meats, and poultry. When they find and enter an airless, low-acid environment, their spores produce vegetative cells that in turn churn out the toxin that kills people.

So why not process low-acid foods in a boiling-water bath? Because unlike molds, yeasts, and enzymes, botulinum spores aren't destroyed or deactivated at the temperature of boiling water. The only—and we mean only—way to destroy botulinum is to process jars of low-acid food in a pressure canner operated at 10 to 15 psi (or pounds per square inch of pressure).

PLAYING IT SAFE

When you fit the facts together, the message is loud and clear. **Never process low-acid foods in a boiling-water bath unless they are pickled.** If you were crazy enough to try, with green beans, for example, you'd be offering any botulinum in the beans the equivalent of a luxury hotel: an environment that is airless (your jars sealed well) and low in acid (lots of tasty beans).

We hope that once you've read this book, you'll never need to think about the symptoms of botulism, but just in case the need arises, the critical symptom to watch for is double vision. If you start seeing ten fingers on each hand, have someone rush you to a hospital for treatment.

UNSAFE CANNING METHODS AND RECIPES

For many decades, home canners used processing methods now known to be unsafe. Some of these canners and their descendants will still swear on their family Bibles that the methods they used were adequate. After all, didn't Great-Aunt Alice (or Jane or Claudia) make delicious canned tomatoes without heat processing the jars at all—and live to boast about it? And didn't Cousin John process his green beans in a boiling-water bath? Great Aunt Alice and Cousin John were very, very lucky. We now know that the methods they used are dangerous.

Described in this section are a few of the unsafe canning methods that you may hear or read about. We include them only because we want to make sure you know how dangerous they are! Unless you feel like playing the home-canning version of Russian roulette, don't use them. Remember that the only two safe processing methods are boiling-water bath processing and pressure canning.

■ *Open-kettle canning* was once the most popular of canning methods. Heated food was placed in scalded jars, and the cooling food created enough of a vacuum to seal the jar lids. The filled jars were never heat processed at all. Although lids will often seal when this method is used, the food in the jars is not safe to eat. Microorganisms can easily enter the jars before you place lids on them, and because the jars are never heat processed, these microorganisms are never destroyed.

■ Canning with aspirin was once rumored to be an effective method of sterilizing food. Aspirin is a very mild form of germicide, but it won't sterilize food or prevent spoilage. Discard any old recipes that list it as an ingredient.

■ Never try to heat process jars in ovens, dishwashers, or microwaves, or on wood stoves. There's no sure way to control the temperatures of these pieces of equipment. In addition, jars may explode in ovens and microwaves.

■ Steam canners are available commercially, but the United States Department of Agriculture (USDA) doesn't recommend these because research on their effects hasn't been adequate.

If you use recipes from older canning books, be sure to check their recommended processing methods and processing times against current information. Scientists have learned so much more about food safety than they knew even ten years ago, that some of these recipes are now outdated and unsafe. You may use the ingredients listed in most of these recipes, but you must adapt the processing methods and times to conform with the information that's provided in the charts on pages 123–26.

Canning Today's Tomato Varieties

Tomatoes, as you probably know, are actually fruits. For years, they were classified as high-acid foods, and home canners often processed them by placing the unheated tomatoes in jars and running them through a boiling-water bath. A few of today's tomato varieties, however, can actually have a pH as high as 4.77, which makes them borderline when it comes to acidity. Rather than take risks when you can tomato recipes, follow the rules offered here:

■ Pressure canning will always provide safer tomato products, but if you want to process tomatoes (crushed or whole) or tomato juice in a boiling-water bath, strengthen their acidity by adding 2 tablespoons of bottled lemon juice or 1/2 teaspoon of citric acid for each quart you plan to can. Four tablespoons of vinegar per quart will also work, but will definitely change the flavor.

■ Always hot pack tomato products (you'll find out how in chapter 3) rather than packing them fresh. Heating the tomatoes before they're placed in jars is a necessary safety precaution.

■ Never attempt to can tomatoes harvested from dead or frost-killed vines, as their acidity strength will be exceptionally low. Keep in mind that green tomatoes are more acidic than ripened fruit.

■ Any mixed-vegetable recipe containing tomatoes, unless the ingredients are pickled, should be processed as a low-acid combination. See page 11 for details.

CANNING AT HIGH ALTITUDES

The recipes in this book and in most books on canning are written for canners whose kitchens are less than 1,000 feet above sea level. High-altitude canners must make some very important adjustments when they sterilize jars for canning and when they heat process food-filled jars. Why? Because the temperature at which water boils decreases as the altitude increases. Microorganisms aren't destroyed by boiling water; they're destroyed by high temperatures. If you live above a certain altitude, the temperature at which your water boils won't be high enough to process food safely.

The adjustments you must make for high-altitude canning are described in the next three paragraphs, but we'll remind you of them repeatedly! Start by finding out the altitude in your location. The Cooperative Extension Service or Soil Conservation Service in your area will be happy to provide this information.

High-Altitude Jar Sterilization

All canning jars must be clean before they're filled with food, but in some cases they must also be sterilized. If the food-filled jars will be processed in a pressure canner or for at least 10 minutes in a boiling-water bath, they don't need to be sterilized. If they'll be processed in a boiling-water bath for fewer than 10 minutes, however, they do need to be sterilized. At sea level, you'll do this by boiling the jars for 10 minutes. At higher altitudes, you must add 1 extra minute of boiling time for every 1,000 feet above sea level. At 6,000 feet, for example, you must boil the jars for 16 minutes.

High-Altitude Boiling-Water Bath Processing

If you live more than 1,000 feet above sea level, your food won't be properly processed in a boiling-water bath unless you add extra processing time to the required times called for in standard recipes. The chart on page 45 provides the adjustments you must make.

High-Altitude Pressure Canning

When a pressure canner is used at sea level and its gauge registers 10 pounds of pressure, you can be certain that the temperature inside the canner is at least 240°F (116°C). When the same canner is used at an elevation of more than 1,000 feet above sea level, however, a 10-pound gauge reading doesn't guarantee as high a temperature. Rather than increase the processing time, as high-altitude canners would when boiling-water bath processing, you must increase the recommended pressure. Use the chart on page 53 as a guide.

MOVING ON

Believe it or not, you've just learned the theories that determine safe home-canning practices. Don't worry if you had some trouble plowing through them. In the next few chapters, you'll learn how to use these theories, and once you've had some experience with them, they'll all fall into place.

CHAPTER 2 setting up

MUCH OF THE EQUIPMENT required for home canning will be in your kitchen already. After reading this chapter, take inventory of what you own. Then, before you start your first canning venture, make sure you stock up on any missing items. You won't have time to dash out for extra jars in the middle of a processing session!

If your budget is tight, consider borrowing any missing items from a friend. There's no reason to invest your hard-earned money in a new hobby until you're sure that it's one you'll enjoy. Another way to limit your initial expenses is to start with recipes that can be safely processed by the boiling-water bath method, as the type of canner required is relatively inexpensive. Purchase a pressure canner when you've saved some extra spending money.

The list that follows includes everything you'll need except a boiling-water bath canner, a pressure canner, and canning jars and lids. These are described on pages 21–25.

EQUIPMENT AND SUPPLIES

■ **Kitchen scales.** These come in especially handy when you're making jams and jellies, as measuring out fruit and sugar accurately helps ensure successful jelling. A scale that will weigh up to 25 pounds is ideal, but a smaller one will work if you weigh the ingredients in batches.

■ **Vegetable brush and a colander.** You'll use these to clean and drain fruits and vegetables.

■ **Stockpots and saucepans.** Many foods are precooked before they're placed in canning jars. Your pots and pans should be made of stainless steel, unchipped enamel, or aluminum. Include at least one very large stockpot and a heavy-bottomed kettle, 8 to 20 quarts in capacity, for making jams and jellies.

■ **Teakettle or large saucepan.** You'll need hot or boiling water to replenish the water in your boiling-water bath canner and to pour over some types of food after packing the food into jars.

■ **High-quality knives, cutting board, and vegetable peeler.** Make sure the knives are made of a metal that won't discolor fresh fruits or vegetables.

■ **Spoons and a ladle.** A good stirring spoon, a slotted spoon for lifting pieces of food from liquid, and a ladle, are all required.

■ **Measuring cups and spoons.** Include a one-quart measuring cup if you can.

■ **Large mixing bowl.** Think in terms of preparing up to seven quarts of food at a time!

■ **Jar funnel.** One end of this special funnel fits just inside the opening of a standard canning jar. The other end is considerably wider, so you can ladle food and liquids into jars without slopping them onto the clean jar rims.

Tips on Equipment and Utensils

■ Utensils and equipment used for canning should be made of stainless steel, enamel-clad metal, or anodized aluminum, or should have a nonstick finish. Don't use utensils made of copper, brass, unlined cast iron, unlined aluminum, or galvanized zinc, as these materials may react with acids and salts, creating unpleasant flavors and colors as a result.

■ For precooking or heating food before you place it in jars, select saucepans or kettles with heavy bottoms so that the heat will disperse evenly throughout the contents.

■ **Lid wand (optional).** Flat, metal jar lids must sit in hot water until you're ready to use them. Lifting them out with tongs is possible, but a lid wand, which has a magnet at one end, saves a lot of time.

■ **Kitchen tongs.** These are handy for lifting pieces of food and, if you don't have a lid wand, for removing lids from hot water.

■ **Bath towel.** Hot jars, just removed from the canner, will crack if they're placed on a cool surface, so place them on a folded bath towel instead.

■ **Air-bubble remover, nonmetallic spatula, or wooden chopstick.** Before fitting lids on filled jars, you must remove air bubbles from the food by running one of these utensils around the jar's interior.

■ **Jar lifter.** This handy contraption operates like a pair of pliers. Its concave jaws provide a perfect grip around canning jars.

■ **Jelly bag and stand (optional).** For some jelly recipes, you must extract juice from cooked fruit, a job made much easier with this slightly ridiculous-looking contraption. A sieve lined with layers of cheesecloth makes an adequate substitute.

■ **Food mill or strainer (optional).** You can always improvise by using cheesecloth or a very fine sieve instead.

■ **Candy thermometer.** Although not absolutely necessary, a thermometer helps determine when jams and jellies have reached the jelling point. Your thermometer must measure temperatures up to 220°F (105°C) and should be marked in 1- or 2-degree graduations. To use the thermometer, position it vertically and crouch down to read it at eye level. Remember not to let its bottom touch the bottom of the pot, or the temperatures registered will be much too high.

- **Labels, either self-adhesive or gummed.** Commercial labels for canning jars, many quite decorative, are available through hardware, grocery, and cookware stores, but some home canners enjoy designing and making their own.

- **Cheesecloth or muslin spice bag.** Used to suspend whole spices in foods as the foods are precooked, these are easy to make. Just cut a circle from several layers of cheesecloth, place the spices in the center of the circle, draw up the edges of the cloth, and tie the bag closed with clean string.

- **Timer.** Keeping track of how long your jars have been processed is critical, so make sure your timer is accurate. A wristwatch or clock with a second hand and alarm will work, too.

- **Notebook, journal, or computer** for recording recipes and the experiences you have while canning them. Keeping records helps save time and money.

Time Savers

Food processors, grinders, slicers, and blenders are so common in today's kitchens that we haven't bothered to list them. These gadgets are all time savers, of course, but if they're too high-priced for you, just remind yourself that superb home-canned foods existed long before high-tech

kitchen equipment! And think about making smaller investments in hand-operated kitchen utensils designed for specific tasks. Apple peelers-and-corers, cabbage slicers, cherry pitters, utensils for slicing corn kernels from the cob, and many more kitchen tools are available through cookware stores and catalogues. We'll admit that we have a real penchant for these, one you'll understand better the first time you spend an entire weekend preparing and canning apple butter or corn relish!

Keeping a Canning Journal

Keeping a canning journal, notebook, or computer file can prove to be immensely helpful in a number of ways.

■ Write down each recipe you prepare so that all your recipes are in a single place.

■ Pretend you're the food critic for a huge newspaper and review the foods you've canned. Delete the recipes that don't satisfy you and make note of the ones that are truly special.

■ Record the date whenever you process a batch of any given recipe. Also write down how many jars you processed and how many you actually eat. Keeping track of what you consume is a great way to prevent waste.

■ For every batch you make of a given recipe, record the varieties of fruits or vegetables you used, and where you purchased those varieties. Next year, you'll know where to look for the produce you want.

BOILING-WATER BATH CANNERS

Boiling-water bath canners, available from many hardware and cookware stores, are large, lidded kettles made specifically for processing jars of high-acid foods.

The typical boiling-water bath canner holds seven one-quart jars or between seven and nine one-pint jars. Some canners will also hold fourteen half-pint jars in two layers. Made of stainless steel, aluminum, or porcelain-coated steel, this type of canner often comes with a metal rack that holds the canning jars away from each other and slightly above the canner's bottom surface. The rack permits boiling water to circulate freely around the jars and helps prevent jars from bumping against each other during processing.

The depth of your boiling-water bath canner is important, so when you shop for one, take along a ruler or measuring tape. A few of the canners on the market today just aren't deep enough for processing quart jars. The food-filled jars must be held slightly above the canner's bottom (the metal rack does this job) and must be covered by 1 to 2 inches of water during processing. The water in the canner must have room—another inch or two—to come to a rolling boil without spilling over onto the stove. A standard quart jar is about 7 inches high, so the canner should be at least 9 inches high in order to process quart jars safely.

PRESSURE CANNERS

Modern pressure canners, which also come with metal racks, are available from many hardware stores and range in size from 4 quarts to 22 quarts in volume capacity. The largest, and from our point of view the best, hold seven one-quart jars. Different models have different lid-sealing and pressure-measurement devices, but most models operate in a similar manner.

The lid of any pressure canner can be locked onto the canner itself to provide an airtight seal. Usually, this seal is made possible by a flexible gasket that fits between the lid and base.

When water is heated in a tightly sealed pressure canner, the steam produced has only one avenue of escape—an opening in the lid known as a *vent port* or *petcock*, depending on the type of canner you're using. When the vent port is covered or the petcock is closed, the pressure and temperature within the canner rise.

How the internal pressure is measured depends on which of the two main types of pressure canner you're using. On a weighted-gauge canner, the pressure is registered by a small round weight with three marks on it (5, 10, and 15 pounds) and three holes in its rim, one under each weight mark. This weight is slipped over the protruding vent port, using the 5-, 10-, or 15-pound

hole, depending upon the amount of pressure required by the food you'll be processing. When the pressure within the canner reaches the correct number of pounds, the weight lets you know by jiggling or rocking back and forth continuously.

On a *dial-gauge canner*, a small dial with a moving needle is built into the lid. The needle indicates the exact internal pressure in 1-pound increments. By watching the needle closely and adjusting the heat as necessary, you can regulate the internal pressure very closely indeed.

Every pressure canner also has a small plug (or safety fuse) built into its lid. If you accidentally allow the pressure in the canner to build up to dangerous levels, the plug will be forced out, and the steam will escape before the canner can explode.

Dial-gauge and weighted-gauge canners are used in much the same manner. Food-filled jars are placed in the canner, along with 2 or 3 inches of hot water. The lid is then locked tightly in place and the vent port is uncovered or the petcock is opened. Next, the canner is heated until steam starts to vent from the petcock or vent port. After all air has vented from the canner, the vent port is covered or the petcock closed in order to pressurize the canner. Once the correct internal pressure has been reached, the gauge or weight is monitored carefully and the heat is adjusted to maintain the correct pressure for the full, recommended processing time.

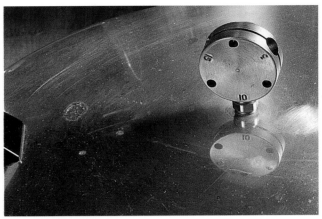

Above: weighted gauge
Below: dial gauge

Cleaning the vent

Maintenance of Pressure Canners

If your canner has a dial gauge, be sure to have the gauge tested for accuracy at least once a year. Using a pressure canner with a defective dial gauge is an invitation to food spoilage and potentially dangerous consequences. Many Cooperative Extension Services will test gauges; those that don't will refer you to the nearest gauge-testing center. It's possible to compensate for errors of up to 1 pound, but we don't recommend it. If your gauge is off, play it safe and buy a new one.

One advantage of weighted-gauge canners is that the weights never need testing. Not much, short of being run over by a two-ton truck, can damage the weighted gauge, but do remember to keep these gauges clean and rust-free.

Check the safety fuse on either type of canner frequently. This small metal or rubber plug should be secure in the lid.

Canner Tips

■ To prevent scale from building up inside boiling-water bath or pressure canners, add 1 tablespoon of distilled white vinegar to the processing water each time you use the canner.

■ To prevent metal racks from rusting, remove them immediately after each canning session and dry them well.

■ Commercial canner racks are not among our favorite objects. They do work for holding jars above the bottom of the canner, but they're also supposed to be useful for loading jars into and out of the canner. We find that many racks are just too flimsy for this job; the jars tend to wobble dangerously in the rack when it's lifted or lowered. Most home canners we know find it easier to move jars with jar lifters.

■ Canner racks are easy to improvise. Round cooling racks work well, and used screw bands (the round bands that cover the flat lids on your jars), fastened together with flexible metal ties, provide a nice, flat surface for the bottoms of the jars.

■ Don't use pressure cookers for pressure canning; they're not interchangeable.

■ Avoid buying a used pressure canner unless you can get your hands on the manufacturer's instruction manual, too. Check the gasket for wear and replace it if necessary. Test the gauge on a used dial-gauge canner right away.

■ It's possible to use a pressure canner for boiling-water bath processing. Make sure the petcock or vent is open or uncovered, and place the lid on the canner without locking it. You don't want any pressure to build up during boiling-water bath processing.

■ If your range is electric, use a canner with a flat bottom, not a ridged bottom, so that heat from the stove element will be distributed evenly. Also make sure that your canner is no more than 4 inches larger in diameter than the diameter of the element.

Check the lid gasket frequently and replace it as soon as it starts to harden, stretch, or crack from use. During processing, watch for steam leaks around the lid, too. If you see any, replace the gasket. Gaskets from older pressure canners may require a light coating of vegetable oil about once a year; on newer models, the gaskets are permanently lubricated by the manufacturer.

Clean the openings in vents and petcocks before each canning session. Just run a pipe cleaner, string, or wire through these narrow openings.

After each use, wash your pressure canner well in hot, soapy water. Then rinse and dry it thoroughly. Also remove, wash, rinse, and dry the lid gasket. To store your pressure canner, place the gasket inside the canner, (not back onto the lid), turn the lid upside down, and place the lid over the canner. Never lock the lid onto a pressure canner between canning sessions.

Recycling Used Jars and Lids

Mason jars with minor nicks and scratches, as well as used lids, come in handy around the home.

■ *Fill a few open jars with fragrant potpourri and set them out around your home.*

■ *Store dried beans, rice, and pastas in slightly defective jars. Lined up in rows on open pantry shelves, these jars not only make up an attractive display, but will help you keep track of when you need to stock up.*

■ *Used jars also make convenient storage containers for odds and ends such as rubber bands, paper clips, and a variety of craft supplies.*

■ *A used Mason jar plays a critical role in maintaining a loving relationship between one of the authors and her three, very spoiled cats. These felines have long preferred to drink water from containers other than their own. For years, the author tried to protect her bedside glass of ice water from their nocturnal marauding by placing a book on top of it. Many spilled glasses and spoiled books later, she finally got the message. She now keeps her own water in a closed thermos, and theirs, complete with ice, in a wide-mouth Mason jar right next to it.*

CANNING JARS

The canning jars that we use today are often called Mason jars. They're named after the nineteenth-century tinsmith, John Landis Mason, who patented the first threaded-rim canning jar that could be sealed with a metal cap and rubber gasket. Several companies now manufacture Mason jars and market them through grocery and hardware stores.

When processing high-acid foods in a boiling-water bath canner, it's possible to substitute used commercial jars, such as those in which mayonnaise is sold, but because these jars aren't manufactured to withstand the stress of home-canning methods, some will break during processing, and some lids (you'll always use new ones) will fail to seal as well. We don't recommend using jars of this type and certainly never in a pressure canner.

Mason jars come in a range of sizes. The most common are ½-pint, 1-pint, 1½-pint, and 1-quart. (Half-gallon jars should be used only for high-acid juices.) Jelly jars are also available in 8-ounce and 12-ounce sizes. New jars are usually sold by the dozen.

The openings of Mason jars vary in size. A standard opening is about 2⅜ inches in diameter, but wide-mouth jars, with 3-inch-diameter openings are also popular, as they make it somewhat easier to pack the jars.

The life span of a canning jar depends almost entirely on how carefully you handle it. As long as you avoid scratching, nicking, or cracking a jar, it can be used over and over again. Before you tackle a day's worth of canning, always check your jars carefully for defects, especially around the upper rim, as an uneven jar rim will prevent the lid from sealing properly. If the jar isn't in perfect condition, don't process food in it.

CANNING LIDS

Closures for canning jars have varied over the years. You've probably seen the old porcelain-lined zinc caps and antique baled-wire lids made of glass. Treat these types of lids as collector's items, but don't use them for your canning needs.

The canning lids manufactured today consist of two parts: a flat, round, metal lid and a metal screw band that is twisted over the lid and onto the threaded neck of the jar. The bottom circumference of the flat lid is slightly flanged and is coated with a sealing compound that rests against the upper rim of the jar. The screw bands are removed after the food is processed, leaving the sealed, flat lid in place on the jar.

Lids come in two sizes, one that fits jars with standard-diameter openings and one to fit wide-mouth jars. You'll find that cardboard cartons of new jars usually include new lids and screw bands as well, but lids with bands may also be purchased separately.

Unless they're rusted or bent, screw bands may be reused, but don't ever use a flat lid twice for canning.

Antique jars and lids

CHAPTER

3

preparing recipes and packing jars

BY THIS TIME, you're probably wondering why we're making you read yet another chapter before you get started. The answer is fairly simple. Many of the steps you'll take as you process your first batch of food involve careful timing, and we'd like to make sure that you don't get stuck in between them. Try to be patient. In the next chapter, you'll finally get a chance to practice what you've learned!

SELECTING PRODUCE

The very first step of any home-canning venture is selecting fine produce. No matter how good your recipe or how carefully you follow correct canning guidelines, starting with overmature, blemished, or bruised fruits and vegetables will yield less than perfect results.

Where to Look

If you're a home gardener or orchardist, you're in luck, of course; you can select what you want to plant and harvest your fruits and vegetables when they're at their peak. Even if you live in a city, however, you can still enjoy delicious canned foods. Start by approaching any gardening friends you have. Not all of them will be home canners, and those who aren't will often harvest more than they can use. Offer to exchange a few jars of home-canned specialty foods in return for a few pounds of fresh produce. Busy gardeners will be delighted by this form of barter.

If you're short on friends with extra produce, visit your local farmers' market. The produce there will be plentiful and probably fresher than what your local supermarket offers. Check with the market sellers to see when they usually replenish their stock. In many areas, sellers restock early on Mondays and Thursdays. Some sellers are also willing to order bulk produce for good customers.

Supermarket produce varies in quality from region to region and store to store. Take the time to compare the produce sections at several stores. Then choose the store you like best and ask the produce manager there when he or she expects to restock depleted vegetable and fruit bins. Plan to do your shopping—and canning, if possible—on that day. We're very fortunate to have an excellent supermarket in our area; we never hesitate to use its produce when our gardens are dormant.

What to Look For

Some varieties of fruits and vegetables are better for canning than others, but these varieties aren't always available throughout the county. Your local Cooperative Extension Service agent is likely to be an invaluable resource in this regard, as she or he will probably be able to recommend the best varieties in your area. Farmers'-market sellers, who often display home-canned produce, are also good resources, but we'd like to offer one bit of advice. If you know which variety you want but can't distinguish one variety from another, shop with some caution. Rather than telling the seller that you're looking for D'Anjou pears, for example, ask for the names of the pear varieties on display. Most sellers are honest and helpful, but a few will tell you whatever you want to hear!

Whether you're purchasing or harvesting vegetables, select young, tender, firm, crisp ones whenever possible, avoiding those that have passed the peak of maturity. Blemished or bruised produce, (see photo at bottom right), is best trimmed and either eaten fresh or cooked and served right away.

If your fruits or vegetables will be processed whole, aim for uniformity of size, choosing beans and cucumbers, for example, of equal thickness and length. For cucumber pickles, use the "burpless," seedless, pickling varieties; they'll stay crisper. Small cucumbers, with their stems still attached, are ideal; you'll often find these at tailgate and farmers' markets.

Most fruits are best for canning when they're fully mature but not overripe. In fact, for jams and jellies without added pectin, about one-quarter of your fruit should be underripe, as underripe fruit is high in natural pectin. (You'll learn more about pectin on pages 102–103.) Process all produce as soon as you can. The fresher it is, the better your finished products will be.

Never used waxed vegetables or fruits. This is especially important in pickled vegetable recipes, as the vinegar-based brine or syrup in these recipes won't penetrate the wax, leaving the vegetables too low in acid to be processed safely in a boiling-water bath.

Handle all produce gently in order not to bruise it and don't wash it until just before you're ready to start canning. Instead, place it in small plastic bags and refrigerate it immediately.

PREPARING JARS AND LIDS

Before you prepare food for canning, check your canning recipe to see how many jars you'll need and what size they should be. Then wash the jars thoroughly by hand in hot, sudsy water and rinse them well, or run them through a dishwasher. (Neither method will sterilize the jars, but a good cleaning is a necessary first step.)

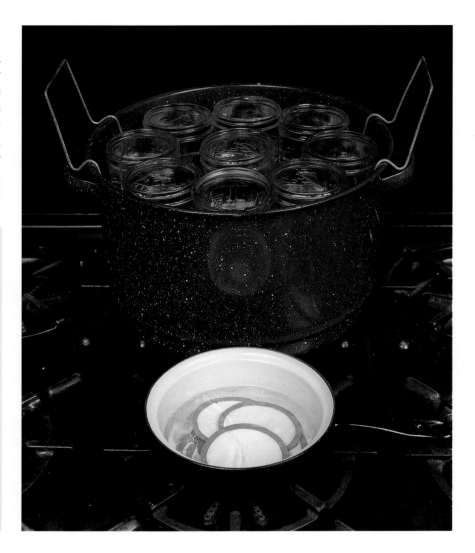

Tips on Jars and Lids

■ If you notice scale in or on clean, used jars, it's probably a result of hard water. Soak the jars for several hours in a solution of 1 cup of vinegar and 1 gallon of water, and then wash them again.

■ Never use a microwave for sterilizing canning jars.

■ Never pour boiling water or place very hot food and liquid into a canning jar that is at room temperature. The stress may cause the jar to crack.

■ Avoid using abrasive materials when washing jars.

Sterilizing Jars

Heat processing will take care of any microorganisms in food-filled jars that are processed in a boiling-water bath for at least ten minutes or that are processed in a pressure canner. Some foods, however, require fewer than ten minutes in a boiling-water bath; jams and jellies are good examples. Jars that you plan to pack with these foods must be sterilized before they're filled.

To sterilize washed and rinsed jars, place them right side up in the rack in your boiling-water bath canner or on a rack in a stockpot large enough to hold them. Add hot (not boiling) water to cover them by at least 1 inch. Then boil the jars for ten minutes. (If you live more than 1,000 feet above sea level, you must add one extra minute of boiling time for each 1,000 feet.) Turn the heat down to low and leave the jars in hot water until you're ready to fill them with food.

Keeping Jars Hot

Both sterilized and unsterilized jars must be kept hot until they're filled. If you wash your jars in the sink, keep them hot by submerging them in hot water in your boiling-water bath canner. If you wash the jars in a dishwasher, leave them inside it, on the hot drying cycle, and remove them one or two at a time when you're ready to fill them.

Cleaning lids

Manufacturers of lids and screw bands provide cleaning instructions for their products. Follow these instructions exactly. Some types of lids and bands must be washed in hot, sudsy water and rinsed. Then the clean lids are placed in a saucepan and covered with water. The water is brought to a simmer (180°F or 82°C), the heat turned off, and the lids left submerged until you're ready to use them. Other types of lids and bands are washed, rinsed, and covered with water that has already been brought to a boil.

PREPARING RECIPES

In chapters 4 and 5, we'll walk you through every step of boiling-water bath processing and pressure canning. Recipes differ, of course, so how you prepare your fruits and vegetables will vary, but a few general rules will almost always apply.

Cleaning Fruits and Vegetables

Food to be canned must be as clean as possible. Wash fruits and vegetables thoroughly, before breaking their skins by paring or slicing them. Larger foods such as pears may be washed under cold running water. Submerge smaller items, such as green beans, in cold water several times, lifting them in handfuls out of the water after each dousing rather than letting the water drain from them while they sit. Use a vegetable brush on firmer produce to remove all traces of dirt. Remember, botulinum bacteria live in the soil, so pay special attention when cleaning root crops such as potatoes. Their nooks and crannies can harbor hidden soil and its residents.

Size of Pieces

In most cases, pieces of food to be canned in the same jar should be equal in size. When you're making whole pickles, for example, select cucumbers that are as close to equal in length and diameter as possible. When making a relish or salsa, chop or dice the ingredients into pieces of similar size. Processing large pieces of food with small ones will prevent heat from permeating the jars' contents evenly.

Herbs and Spices

When preparing foods for canning, many cooks prefer to use fresh herbs and whole spices, as dried, powder herbs and spices darken processed foods considerably. Because jars filled with floating herbs and spices can be unsightly, it's best to place these flavorful additions in a muslin or cheese-cloth spice bag. Their flavor is imparted to the food or syrup as the food is precooked.

Preventing Discoloration

If you've ever taken a bite out of a fresh apple and then left it on a counter when the phone rang, you'll know that the flesh of some fruits quickly discolors when it's exposed to the air. Apricots, pears, peaches, cherries, and grapes are especially vulnerable, as are potatoes and mushrooms. Remember those enzymes? To prevent them from going to work on peeled and/or sliced produce, you must use an antioxidant solution.

Working rapidly and in small batches, peel and slice the fruit, and drop each piece into a bowl filled with one of the following preparations:

■ A solution made up of 1 gallon of water and 1 teaspoon (about 3 grams) of ascorbic acid powder or 6 crushed 500-milligram Vitamin C tablets.

■ A commercial antioxidant. You'll find this powdered product on the canning-supply shelves of hardware and grocery stores. The small jars come with preparation instructions.

Try not to leave the food in any of these solutions for longer than 15 minutes, or the taste of the solution may linger. Just before packing the food into your canning jars, drain it thoroughly and then rinse it well under cold running water.

PACKING JARS

Once you've prepared your food, you must transfer it to your canning jars, a process known as *packing*. Then you must place lids and screw bands on the jars before the jars are heat processed.

Raw Packing and Hot Packing

Canning jars are filled in one of two ways. In the first method, known as *raw packing*, unheated food is placed in clean, hot canning jars and then covered with hot water, hot juice, or hot syrup that has been brought to a boil and cooled slightly. After the lids are fastened to the jars with screw bands, the jars are placed in a canner containing hot—not boiling—water. (Placing warm jars in boiling water can cause them to crack.)

The raw-pack method is usually used with delicate foods such as whole peaches, which tend to soften significantly when they're precooked before being heat processed. This method does save preparation time, as you don't have to precook the food, and it does preserve some of the food's nutritional value, but it also has disadvantages. The jars will hold less, as the fresh food in them will shrink during processing. (Packing the food fairly tightly, without crushing the pieces, will help compensate for this fact.) Processed raw-packed foods also retain more air than processed precooked foods, so you may find that the pieces of processed food float to the tops of the jars. In addition, air in processed foods is likely to cause color changes after two to three months of storage. You'll also notice that after processing and cooling, the liquid and food level in raw-packed jars sometimes lowers.

Hot-packed foods, unlike raw-packed foods, are brought to a boil and simmered for a few minutes before they're placed in the jars. The hot food is then covered with boiling water, syrup, or the liquid in which the food was cooked.

Although hot-packed foods require extra preparation time and can lose some nutritional value and texture during precooking, this method is often recommended. Softened, precooked food is much easier to pack into jars, and because the food shrinks during precooking, more will fit into each jar. Processed, hot-packed foods also contain less air than raw-packed foods, so they're less likely to float in the jar and more likely to retain their colors and flavors.

Each of the recipes in this book specifies which packing method to use, and the chart on pages 123-26 includes a column that offers specifications for particular fruits and vegetables. Always follow these recommendations closely.

Leaving Headspace

When filling clean Mason jars with prepared food, you must leave a space between the top of the food and the rim of the jar. Known as *headspace*, this gap allows the food and liquid in the jar to move about during heat processing. If you don't leave enough headspace, the contents of the jars may force themselves out during processing, spoiling the seals between lids and jars as they do. Leaving too much headspace may also cause sealing failures because the recommended processing time won't be sufficient to force all the extra air out of the jars.

Different types of food require different amounts of headspace; some foods expand more than others when heated. In general, low-acid foods, such as corn and peas, require 1 to 1¼ inches of headspace; fruits, which are high acid, require ½ inch; and juices, jellies, pickles, and relishes require only ¼ inch. You'll find recommended headspaces provided in our canning recipes and in the chart on pages 123–26.

Placing Lids on Jars

After you've packed a jar, you must remove any trapped air in the food by running a narrow spatula or wooden chopstick around the inside of the jar and up and down through the ingredients. (You may have to add more liquid afterwards to adjust the headspace.) Then wipe off the rim of the jar with a clean, damp cloth or paper towel to help ensure a good seal between the jar and lid.

Next, using a lid wand or kitchen tongs, lift a lid from the hot water and place it on top of the rim of the jar. Twist down a screw band over the lid. Here's a tip on tightening screw bands: Twist the band until you first feel resistance and then continue turning it for another 1½ inches.

When all the jars have been filled and the lids and bands are in place, the jars are ready for heat processing in either a boiling-water bath canner or pressure canner, depending upon the ingredients.

Correct headspace is very important.
The right-hand jar does not contain enough liquid.

HEAT PROCESSING

In the next two chapters, you'll find step-by-step instructions for boiling-water bath processing and pressure canning. Practice each method by using the simple recipes in these chapters. When processing other recipes in this book, follow the recipe's recommendations as to the length of processing time and, if the food must be pressure canned, the required pounds of pressure. These time and pressure guidelines have been carefully calculated to ensure that your canned food will be safe to eat; don't vary them!

PATTI HILL (shown basking beneath the many ribbons she's won from state and county fairs) is a basket maker, weaver, retired restaurant owner, gardener, and motorcyclist. She's also a "master canner"—a designation offered to people in our county who complete the excellent course in home canning offered by our Cooperative Extension Service. Her home-canned foods have won more ribbons than the walls of her pantry can display. Even more impressive is the fact that she's willing to share her winner's tips with other canners.

When we interviewed Patti at her home, she made the point that judges are often swayed as much by the appearance of a jar and its contents as by the quality of the food itself. To demonstrate her point, she showed us the jars of beans on the opposite page. The two jars of plain green beans will taste exactly the same, as will the two jars of dilled beans, but the jars at the rear were prepared and packed "family-style," while the jars at the front were packed to win ribbons.

The beans in the family-style jar to the right are roughly the same thickness and length and were ladled into the jar quickly. Now look at the prize-winning jar in front, which Patti packed to please the judges! She started by carefully selecting beans that were equal in thickness. Then she cut them to exactly the same angles and lengths. When she was ready to pack the jar, she placed it on its side and packed the beans one at a time, placing each one at an angle. She was just as careful packing her prize-winning "dilly" beans. She set the jar on its side, and packed it in layers, starting with the two cloves of garlic and a spray of dill. She slipped the beans in horizontally, one by one, so they'd stand straight up-and-down when the jar was turned upright.

The judges also loved Patti's tomatoes, and she knows why. Take a look at the tomato jars in the photo to the right. The one in front, with the perfectly shaped, whole Roma tomatoes, won a ribbon in the North Carolina State Fair. Here's how Patti prepared it. First, she preheated enough tomatoes to fill seven hot-packed, quart jars. Most of the tomatoes reacted by bursting as they got hot. These, Patti packed into family-style jars. The few tomatoes that remained whole, she carefully ladled into her prize-winning jar, because judges prefer whole tomatoes to tomato pieces.

The applesauce jars shown in the same photo serve as yet another example of how important appearance can be at the fair. The kind of applesauce that Patti makes for herself is hearty,

Winning Blue Ribbons

swimming with tasty apple chunks and dark with spices. The kind that she makes for the judges, however, is fine-textured and almost white. (Patti takes the same careful approach with jellies and preserves. She strains the pulp from the juice she uses in jellies and avoids floating fruit in her preserves by fitting as many pieces of fruit into her jars as possible.)

On the assumption that the judges can only appreciate what they can actually see, Patti also avoids using highly decorative jars, the surfaces of which are sometimes so heavily patterned that the contents aren't visible. She's always careful to use new lids and rust-free canning rings.

Quality does make a difference, of course, and the judges will always taste the contents of your jars. They also insist upon knowing how the food was prepared, so Patti attaches a label to each jar, listing the contents, the heat-processing method used, and the processing time and/or pressure. She's careful to put the label on top of the jar, so as not to obstruct the view of the food.

All jars must be prepared using safe and accepted procedures. (You'll find them described in this book.) Patti also refers to fair premium books to familiarize herself with all the factors that the judges consider: color, liquid, shape, clarity, texture, consistency, appearance, appropriate size, pack, and jar fill. She recalls one particularly competitive fair, in which the headspace at the top of the jar was the tie-breaking factor.

Although Patti has a store of ribbons and loves to win, she's quick to point out that meeting people and sharing information about the "art of canning" are the reasons she enters fairs. She loves the spirit of friendly competition and finds entering her canned goods in the local fair educational, rewarding, and—above all—fun!

4 boiling-water bath processing

AS YOU NOW KNOW, high-acid foods (fruits and pickled foods) are processed in a boiling-water bath canner. The steps involved are really quite simple, but they do involve some careful planning, so before you begin, take the time to read this chapter carefully.

We've chosen a recipe—hot-packed spiced pears in a light sugar syrup—that is simple but delicious. Once you've canned these pears, you'll know how to process any high-acid food by the same method.

Starting Tips

■ If you live at an altitude of over 1,000 feet above sea level, be sure to refer to the chart on page 45 and adjust your processing times accordingly.

■ We used red D'Anjou pears in this example, as they retain their firm texture after processing. Select firm pears that are roughly equal in size and fully ripe but not overripe. Cull out any that are bruised, blemished, or underripe, and save them for slicing and eating fresh.

■ Adding ½ cup of distilled white vinegar to the water in the canner each time you use it will help prevent the buildup of scale on jar exteriors and inside the canner.

■ We used wide-mouth jars for our pears, but standard-mouth jars will work just as well if you cut your pears to a size that will fit through their openings. Just make sure you have lids to match!

■ Our pear recipe yields seven pints. If you'd like to process nine jars at one time, remove the metal rack from your canner and make one out of screw bands instead (see page 23). The metal rack holds only seven jars comfortably, but a homemade rack will allow you to fit in two more one-pint jars. If you plan to process nine jars, however, remember never to wedge them in tightly, as the water in the canner must be able to circulate freely among all the jars. Also remember to increase the ingredient quantities accordingly.

■ As you prepare your food and pack the jars, keep an eye on the water preheating in your canner (see step 2). The difference in temperature between the water and these hot-packed jars of pears mustn't be too great, or the jars may crack as they're lowered into the canner. The water should be simmering, but not boiling, when you're ready to load the jars. (For raw-packed jars, the water in the canner should be hot rather than simmering.)

■ The spiced pears in this recipe are processed for 20 minutes, so you needn't sterilize your clean jars. (For information on sterilizing jars, see page 30.)

Lightly Spiced Pears

YIELD: **7 pints**
PACK: **Hot**
HEADSPACE: **½ inch**
PROCESSING TIME: **20 minutes**

INGREDIENTS

8½–9 pounds pears
4½ cups water
1 cup plus 2 tablespoons sugar
2 cinnamon sticks, broken into pieces
12 whole cloves

METHOD

1 Clean all utensils and work surfaces thoroughly and arrange all utensils so they'll be on hand when you need them. You won't have time to waste looking for jar lifters or a lid wand once you've started!

2 Make sure the metal rack is in your canner. Place the canner on the stove and pour enough water into it to cover the pint jars by 1 to 2 inches once the jars are in place. Place the lid on the canner, turn the heat to high, and start preheating the water-filled canner. Also preheat extra water in a teakettle or saucepan; you may need to add boiling water to your canner once the filled jars are in it.

3 Check your jars carefully for nicks, cracks, or scratches, setting any damaged jars aside. Running one finger around the rim of the jar is an easy way to detect imperfections.

4 If you own a dishwasher, run the jars through it, leaving them inside to keep them hot until you're ready to fill them. If you don't own a dishwasher, first wash the jars by hand in hot, soapy water and rinse them thoroughly. Then lift the lid from the canner and use tongs or a jar lifter to carefully lower each jar into the preheated water. Tilt the jars slightly as you do this, or you may be splashed by scalding water.

5 Following the manufacturer's instructions (they'll differ from brand to brand), wash and rinse the lids and screw bands. Some instructions call for placing the clean lids in a saucepan, bringing the water to a simmer, and then removing the saucepan from the heat, leaving the lids submerged until you're ready to use them. Other manufacturers recommend pouring boiling water over the lids and letting them stand in this water.

6 Weigh the pears (8½ to 9 pounds) if you haven't already done so. You don't want to prepare too few or too many.

7 Before breaking the skins of the pears, wash them well under cold running water. A vegetable brush will help remove dirt from crannies.

8 In a large mixing bowl or food-grade plastic pail, prepare an antioxidant solution to keep the pears from turning brown. If you use the commercial antioxidant powder commonly sold with canning supplies, just follow the manufacturer's instructions for preparation. A solution may also be made by dissolving either one teaspoon (about 3 grams) of ascorbic acid powder or six crushed 500-milligram Vitamin C tablets in one gallon of water. (We actually prepared about 1½ gallons for the pears in this recipe.)

9 Working quickly, cut each pear into halves or quarters, coring and peeling each piece of fruit and dropping it into the antioxidant solution right away. As you can see in the photo above, we accidentally dropped an unpeeled quarter into the solution. Our mistake!

10 In a large saucepan, combine 4½ cups of water and 1 cup plus 2 tablespoons of sugar. Wrap the cinnamon-stick pieces and cloves in muslin or cheesecloth and tie the fabric closed with clean string. Drop the bag into the saucepan, leaving one end of the string draped over the rim of the pan or tying it to one handle.

11 Drain the pear pieces, rinse them under cold running water, and add them to this mixture. Boil the pears and syrup for 5 minutes. Then turn the heat down slightly. The pears and syrup must stay hot as you fill the jars, but they shouldn't be overcooked.

12 Using jar lifters, remove a hot jar from the canner, carefully pouring the water in it back into the canner. Place the hot jar on a surface that isn't so cool it will crack the jar. You may also want to use a thermometer to check the water temperature in the canner at this point. For these hot-packed jars, the water temperature should be about 180°F (82°C) when you place the filled jars in the canner. When working with raw-packed jars, the temperature should be about 150°F (66°C).

13 To help keep the jar rim clean, fit a jar funnel into its opening. Using a slotted spoon or kitchen tongs, pack the jar with hot pears, leaving about ½ inch of headspace. (Pear halves may not fit through the funnel opening; just remove the funnel if you have this problem.) Avoid packing the pieces of fruit too tightly, or the syrup won't be able to circulate among them, and uneven heating will result. If spicy flavors please you, add a small piece of cinnamon stick or a few whole cloves to each jar.

14 Ladle the hot syrup into the jar funnel until ½ inch of headspace remains at the top of the jar. Remove the funnel when you're through.

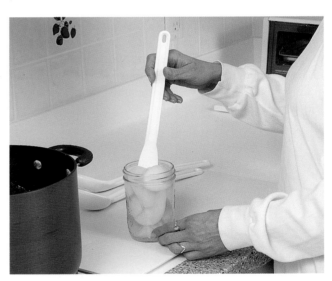

15 To remove any air bubbles in the jar, run an air-bubble remover, a nonmetallic spatula, or a wooden chopstick around the inside of the jar, moving the implement up and down as you do. Check the headspace again when you're through and add more syrup if necessary to bring the headspace back up to ½ inch.

16 With a clean, damp cloth or a dry paper towel, carefully wipe the rim and threads of the jar. These portions of the jar must be clean, or the lid won't seal properly.

17 Using a lid wand, tongs, or a fork, carefully lift a lid from the saucepan of hot water and center it over the clean rim of the jar. Keep your fingers away from the underside of the lid and rim of the jar; they must remain as clean as possible.

18 Place a screw band over the lid. To tighten the screw band properly, first turn it until you feel it begin to resist you, then twist it another 1½ inches. Bands that are too tight will trap air in the jars as they're processed, and the air will spoil the seals by causing the lids to buckle upward. Bands that are too loose won't hold the lids down on the jars at all; food and liquid may be forced out of the jars, which will also spoil the seals.

19 Check the water in the canner to make sure it's simmering. (When processing raw-packed jars, you may need to bring down the water temperature in order to prevent the jars from cracking when you lower them into the canner. Just add cold water to the canner as necessary.) Using jar lifters, lower the filled jar into the canner until it rests on the rack. Then pack the remaining jars, placing each one in the canner after its lid and screw band are in place.

20 If the jars in the canner aren't covered by at least 1 inch of water, add simmering water from your tea kettle. Take care not to pour this directly onto the jars, or they may crack. (For raw-packed jars, add hot rather than simmering water.)

21 Place the lid on the canner and turn the heat up high. It may take up to 30 minutes to bring the water to a vigorous boil, but don't get impatient! Heat processing in a boiling-water bath canner doesn't actually start until a full boil has been reached.

22 When—and not until—the water in the canner reaches the full-boil stage, set your timer for 20 minutes. (If you live more than 1,000 feet above sea level, you'll need to add extra time. (See the chart on page 45.)

23 After you've set your timer, you'll probably need to lower the heat slightly in order to maintain a steady, but gentle boil. Be careful, though: If the water temperature falls below the boiling point, bring the water back to a boil and reset your timer for the full processing time, which is 20 minutes for these pears. Keep an eye on the water level, too. You may need to add boiling water from your kettle in order to keep the jars covered by 1 or 2 inches at all times.

24 As soon as the recommended heat-processing time is up, turn off the heat. Carefully remove the canner lid, tilting it away from you in order to avoid steam burns. And remember: Don't ever be tempted to cut down on the processing time in the canner; these times are scientifically gauged to protect you!

25 Using a jar lifter, remove the jars from the canner right away and place them on a dry, folded bath towel or wooden board, at least 1 inch apart from one another, in a draft-free area. Allowing the jars to sit in the canner too long will result in overprocessed food. Avoid letting the jars contact anything cold or damp, or they may crack. Don't tamper with the lids; leave any loose screw bands just as they are. Tightening the bands at this point may ruin the seals. Allow the water in the canner to cool for an hour or two before emptying it.

26 Allow the jars to cool untouched for 12 to 24 hours. You may very well hear the lids sealing during this time. The vacuum created within each jar as the pears cool will suck the lid downward; you'll hear a distinctive pinging sound as the lid snaps into its sealed, concave position.

27 When the jars are cool, remove the screw bands and dry them well before storing them for re-use. The bands serve no purpose once the lids have sealed and will only be likely to rust or corrode if they're left in place. If you run into a stubborn screw band, don't force it off. Soak a rag in very hot water, ring it out, and wrap it around the band for a couple of minutes. The heat should expand the band and make it easier to remove.

28 Before storing the jars, you must check their seals. A good seal is usually easy to see; the lid will be slightly indented in its center. To check, press down gently on each lid with a thumb or finger. If the lid doesn't give at all, the jar has sealed. If the lid dips down and stays down when you lift your finger or thumb, the seal will probably be fine, although you may want to mark this jar when you label it so that you'll remember to check its seal especially carefully before opening it.

If the lid springs back up again when you lift your finger or thumb, the jar hasn't sealed properly. Another way to identify an inadequate seal is to turn the jar upside down and look for obvious leaks or less obvious air bubbles rising from the lid through the pears. A continuous stream of tiny bubbles indicates that air is entering the jar. If you find any jars that haven't sealed properly, either refrigerate the pears and eat them within a few days or reprocess them immediately, using another clean jar, in case the old one had a defective rim or threads, and a new lid. Don't forget to add hot syrup or boiling water, if necessary, to compensate for any liquid that may have leaked from the jar. Reprocess for a full 20 minutes.

29 Remove the screw bands and wipe the sealed jars well with a hot, soapy cloth. Then rinse and dry them thoroughly. This step isn't just a matter of aesthetics! If you take the time to clean your jars before arranging them on a pantry shelf, and if you later find that one of these jars has traces of food on its exterior, you'll know that the seal has broken during storage and that the food isn't safe to eat.

30 Label each jar with the name of the recipe and with the processing date. We also include the number of the journal page where we've recorded the recipe, the pear varieties we've tried with it, our "reviews," and useful tips and reminders.

31 Store the sealed jars in a cool, dry, dark place. See page 55 for details.

Processing Multiple Batches

Once you know all the stages of boiling-water bath canning by heart, you'll be ready to try processing multiple batches. Just schedule a day without interruptions, line up four boiling-water bath canners, and make sure you have enough jars and lids.

Start by filling the four canners with water and preheating them. Unless you'd prefer to use a dishwasher, you'll use one of these canners—we'll call it "canner X"—for keeping washed and rinsed jars hot. Wash at least two sets of jars and place the first set in canner X.

Prepare the first batch of your recipe. Then, each time you take a jar out of canner X to fill it with prepared food, replace it with another clean jar so that canner X is always filled with empty jars.

As the jars in the first batch are being processed in one of the other canners, wash more jars, and prepare the next recipe.

Continue to replace the jars in canner X with new, clean ones as you gradually fill the other three canners with packed jars.

When the three other canners have been filled, just remove the last jars from canner X, pack them, and return them to canner X for processing. If you'd like to process more than four batches, reserve canner X for keeping the jars hot, and use the other three canners, filling them again as you remove each processed batch. As long as the water in the canners remains clean, by all means use it to process subsequent batches. Just add more water as necessary.

You may use this method for pressure canning, too, but not with weighted-gauge canners. You'd never be able to keep track of which weights were jiggling or rocking and which weren't. The din would be too confusing!

BOILING-WATER BATH PROCESSING AT HIGH ALTITUDES

The higher the altitude at which you live, the thinner the air. Why is this important? Because the thinner the air is, the lower the temperature at which water will boil. If you live more than 1,000 feet above sea level, your food won't be properly processed in a boiling-water bath unless you add extra processing time. The chart to the right provides the adjustments you'll need to make.

Altitude Adjustments for Boiling-Water Bath Processing

Altitude in Feet	Increase Processing Time by
1,001-3,000	5 minutes
3,001-6,000	10 minutes
6,001-8,000	15 minutes
8,001-10,000	20 minutes

Sugar in Canned Fruit

Traditional recipes for canned fruits almost always call for heavy, sugar-based syrups. Today, many health- and weight-conscious home canners prefer syrups that aren't as cloyingly sweet or as high in calories. Although sugar plays a critical role in jam and jelly making, in ordinary canned fruits, while it does help to retain color, texture, and flavor, it isn't a critical ingredient.

In the chart that follows, you'll find sugar-to-water ratios for syrups ranging from very sweet indeed to one that is almost sugarless. Consult your sweet tooth (and conscience) before selecting the syrup you'd like to make.

For a Seven-Quart Batch

	AMT. OF WATER	AMT. OF SUGAR
Very light syrup	10½ cups	1¼ cups
Light syrup	9 cups	2¼ cups
Medium syrup	8¼ cups	3¼ cups
Heavy syrup	7¾ cups	5¼ cups
Very heavy syrup	6½ cups	6¾ cups

In general, each pint of canned fruit requires about 1/2 to 3/4 cup of liquid, whether that liquid consists of sugar syrup, unsweetened fruit juice, or water. Each quart requires 1 to 1-1/2 cups. Use soft water if possible, as the minerals in hard water may darken canned foods or turn them gray.

If refined white cane or beet sugar isn't one of your favorite ingredients, you may substitute either corn syrup or honey for up to one-half of the sugar in a syrup recipe, or maple syrup for up to one-quarter of the sugar. Do be sure to select a light-colored corn syrup or very mild-flavored honey, or you'll end up drowning the fruit's natural flavor. Strong-flavored sweeteners such as sorghum and molasses will overwhelm the natural fruit flavor completely. Brown sugar will darken your product, but we sometimes include it for its special flavor.

As a substitute for sugar-based syrups, you may also use unsweetened fruit juice (preferably juice from the same type of fruit you're canning) or even plain water. Do keep in mind that fruit canned in water will be softer in texture than fruit processed in syrup. Select extra firm, fully ripe fruit and hot pack the jars, boiling the fruit in the juice or water first. Add extra boiling water or juice if necessary to adjust the headspace and process the jars in the usual manner.

Artificial sweeteners lose their sweetness during heat processing and can leave a slightly bitter, metallic aftertaste as well. We avoid using them in our recipes.

CHAPTER 5 pressure canning

THOSE OF YOU who remember the old pressure cookers (the ones that struck fear into every sensible cook's heart) should start this chapter by letting go of any lingering cowardice. Today's pressure canners are entirely safe to use. It's a good thing, too. Canning low-acid foods (vegetables, meat, poultry, seafood, soups, and mushrooms) by any other method just isn't acceptable. Only a pressure canner can render temperatures of 240°F to 250°F (115°C to 121°C), and only temperatures this high will destroy the bacteria that love low-acid foods and airless environments.

Starting Tips

■ If you live at an altitude of more than 1,000 feet above sea level, be sure to refer to the chart on page 53 and adjust your processing pressures accordingly. Don't forget that at high altitudes, if you use a weighted-gauge canner rather than a dial-gauge canner, you must increase the pressure in 5-pound increments.

■ Always inspect your pressure canner before using it (see pages 22–23), cleaning its vent port or petcock opening thoroughly and making sure, if the canner has a dial gauge, that the gauge has been checked for accuracy. If you're using a brand-new pressure canner, and if you're a beginner, read the manufacturer's instructions and follow them to the letter.

■ For pressure canning, select vegetables that are as fresh as possible; make sure they're not overripe. Tender, fresh, young green beans are best. Sort the beans by size and degree of maturity, setting aside any that are bruised or rusted. Also cull out any beans that are so mature they're nearly at "shell-out" stage. (Canning very mature beans is possible, but you must increase the processing time by 20 minutes when you do.)

■ Many recipes for processed vegetables, especially older recipes, call for salt, but we've omitted it here. Salt isn't necessary as a preservative in pressure-canned foods other than pickles and actually breaks down the textures of canned vegetables. For more information on salt, turn to the next page.

■ We chose green beans as our model for pressure canning low-acid foods because we wanted to show you the differences between raw packing and hot packing. Raw-packed and hot-packed green beans are processed for the same amount of time, so all we had to do was pack a few jars of each and process them together. As you carry out the instructions in this chapter, hot pack your beans. You'll be glad you did!

■ Although we used a dial-gauge canner to process our beans, the step-by-step instructions in this chapter will show you how to use a weighted-gauge canner as well. Both types of canners are shown on the opposite page.

Green Beans

YIELD: **7 pints**
PACK: **Raw or Hot**
HEADSPACE: **1 inch**
DIAL-GAUGE CANNER TIME & PRESSURE: **20 minutes/11 pounds**
WEIGHTED-GAUGE CANNER TIME & PRESSURE: **20 minutes/10 pounds**

INGREDIENTS
7½ pounds green snap beans

METHOD

1 Clean all utensils and work surfaces thoroughly. Then assemble and arrange everything you'll need so that you don't waste critical time searching for missing items.

2 Pour 2 to 3 inches of water into the bottom of the pressure canner and begin preheating this water.

3 Check your Mason jars carefully for nicks, cracks, or scratches, setting any damaged jars aside.

4 Either run the jars through a dishwasher, where you can keep them hot until you need them, or wash and rinse them by hand and keep them hot in a preheated, water-filled boiling-water bath canner or stockpot. Preheat a kettle of water to pour over the raw-packed beans once you've packed them into the jars. (You don't need to sterilize jars that will be processed in a pressure canner.)

5 Wash, rinse, and prepare the two-piece lids and screw bands according to the manufacturer's instructions.

6 Wash the green beans well by submerging them in cold water several times. Lift them out of each rinse rather than letting the water drain from them while they sit. You don't want remaining particles of soil to cling to them.

Salt

Salt is a required ingredient in some foods. In traditional brined pickles and sauerkraut, which we don't cover in this book, it's critical, as it helps form the lactic acid bacteria that acts as a pickle preservative and also adds flavor and crispness. In seafood recipes and cured or smoked foods, it also serves necessary preservative functions. In home-canned vegetables, meat, and poultry, however, salt doesn't act as a preservative and doesn't affect processing times, color, or texture either. Many older canning recipes for canned vegetables list salt as matter of course, but you may always omit it if you like, salting the food when you serve it instead.

When you do use salt, whether you're making quick pickles or adding optional salt to vegetables, always use canning, pickling, or kosher salt, not the table salt that you purchase in round containers from the grocery store. The latter type of salt, while it's safe to include, contains noncaking materials that will make pickles and vegetables cloudy. We don't recommend flake salt, either; it's not consistently dense, so measuring it accurately by tablespoons or cups is almost impossible. One further tip: When using kosher salt, be sure to weigh it rather than measuring it by volume, as it's extremely coarse.

We avoid using commercial salt substitutes in processed foods, as they change the flavor and texture of the food noticeably and can also create unattractive cloudiness in liquids. If you're on a reduced-sodium diet, add some zest to your recipes by including lemon or orange juice, a bit of citrus peel, or herbs and spices such as mace, nutmeg, or curry powder. If you like, you can substitute reduced-sodium salt for pickling salt in quick-pickle recipes.

7 Trim away the ends of the beans, and slice the beans into pieces about 1 inch long. You may pack whole beans if you wish. Just make sure they're at least 1¼ inches shorter than the height of the jar so that they'll be covered by liquid.

8 To prepare green beans for hot packing, place them in a stockpot large enough to hold them, cover them with water, bring the water to a boil, and boil the beans for 5 minutes.

9 Using jar lifters, remove a hot jar from the dishwasher, stockpot, or boiling-water bath canner. Place a jar funnel over the jar. To pack the hot beans into the jar, use a slotted spoon or tongs to remove them from the boiling liquid and insert them through the funnel. Pack the jar tightly enough not to waste space but loosely enough to permit liquid to flow around the bean pieces.

10 Using a ladle, pour boiling cooking liquid over the beans, leaving 1 inch of headspace.

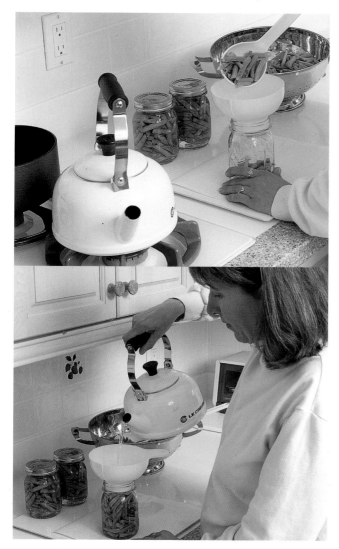

11 If you'd like to experiment by raw packing a jar, fill it with fresh bean pieces instead of cooked ones. Pack these fairly firmly, as they'll shrink considerably during processing. Cover the raw-packed beans with boiling water from your kettle.

12 To eliminate any air bubbles in the jar, run an air-bubble remover, a nonmetallic spatula, or a wooden chopstick around the inside of the jar, moving the implement up and down as you do. When you're through, add more boiling cooking liquid (or boiling water) if necessary to bring the headspace back up to 1 inch.

13 With a clean, damp rag or paper towel, carefully wipe the rim and threads of the jar. These portions of the jar must be clean, or the lid won't seal properly.

14 Using a lid wand or tongs, lift a lid from the saucepan of water and center it over the clean rim of the jar. Place a screw band over the lid and tighten it by hand.

15 Using jar lifters, put the filled jar into the pressure canner, setting it on the rack in the bottom. Then repeat to fill the remaining jars and place them in the canner.

16 Place the lid on the pressure canner and fasten it securely, following the manufacturer's instructions to lock it down. If you see any steam escaping from around the lid during processing, you've either failed to lock the lid in place, or the lid gasket is defective. In either case, your food will not be processed correctly.

17 If you're using a dial-gauge canner, make sure the petcock is open. (This is the small, hollow tube protruding from the lid.) If you're using a weighted-gauge canner, leave the weighted gauge off the vent port. Turn the heat to high. As the water inside the canner heats, air and steam will begin to escape upward through the open petcock or vent port. As soon as you see this happening, set your timer for 10 minutes. Every time you use your pressure canner, you must allow it to vent in this fashion in order to force all the air out. (Follow the manufacturer's recommendations as to venting time.) If any air remains in the canner during processing, temperatures in the canner will be too low—even when the correct pressure has been reached—to process your food correctly. This is a special problem with dial-gauge canners, which unlike weighted-gauge canners, don't continue to vent during the actual processing.

18 After the canner has vented for 10 minutes, close the petcock by placing the counterweight over it. If you're using a weighted-gauge canner, just slip the weight over the vent port, making sure that the number 10 is at the top of the weight when the weight is in place. The pressure inside the canner will rise over the next 3 to 5 minutes.

As you can see in the photo above, our dial-gauge canner has a special lid-locking mechanism, with a button that pops up as soon as the pressure in the canner rises high enough to operate it. This same button drops back down when pressure in the canner decreases as it cools.

19 When the dial gauge indicates that the pressure has reached 11 pounds, set your timer for 20 minutes. If you're using a weighted-gauge canner, the weight will begin to jiggle or rock when the internal pressure reaches 10 pounds. You may need to turn the heat down slightly to maintain the correct pressure for the full length of the processing time.

20 Continue to watch the dial-gauge closely—or listen to the weighted gauge as it jiggles or rocks. The canner must maintain an even pressure, as fluctuating pressures may draw liquids from the jars, destroying the seals in the process. If an emergency draws you away from the stove and the pressure drops while you're gone, bring it back up again by turning up the heat, and when the correct pressure has been reached, start timing all over again for a full 20 minutes.

Remember that heat processing canned foods for the full, recommended length of time (and at the correct pressure when you're using a pressure canner) is absolutely critical. Processing times should never be shortened or interrupted and then completed later. Keep an eye on your canner as it does its job. If the pressure falls below the required level, don't just bring it back up to the required specifications and finish off the remaining time. Start all over again! The food won't be safe to eat unless the canner maintains the correct pressure for the full length of time.

21 When the jars have been processed for the required length of time (in this case, 20 minutes), turn the heat off. If possible, remove the pressure canner from the burner or heating element.

22 Allow the canner to rest undisturbed until the pressure has returned to zero. Never attempt to cool the canner quickly, by holding it under running water, for example, or your food may spoil.

23 When the gauge indicates that there's no more pressure in the canner, open the petcock by removing the counterweight (or remove the weighted gauge from the vent port) and allow another 2 minutes to pass. Then—carefully and slowly—remove the lid, tilting it away from you so that you aren't burned by any residual steam.

24 Using jar lifters, remove the jars and place them upright on a clean folded towel, leaving plenty of space around each jar.

25 Now's the time to study the difference between raw-packed and hot-packed beans. Take a look at the jars above. As you can see, the beans in the raw-packed jar shrank during processing. Notice, too, that there are fewer beans and more liquid in the raw-packed jar and that the raw-packed beans tend to float. This is because they contain more air than the beans which were precooked. The hot-packed beans, which shrank during precooking, fill the jar evenly and completely.

26 Allow the jars to cool undisturbed for 12 to 24 hours. Then follow steps 27 through 31 on page 44 to remove the screw bands and test the seals, and to wash, label, and store the jars.

PRESSURE CANNING AT HIGH ALTITUDES

Altitude in Feet	Pounds Pressure (psi)	
	Dial-Gauge Canner	Weighted-Gauge Canner
1–1,000	11	10
1,001–2,000	11	15
2,001–4,000	12	15
4,001–6,000	13	15
6,001–8,000	14	15
8,001–10,000	15	15

Note that the adjustment you'll need to make is in the pressure, not in the recommended processing time. The latter will stay the same for the specific food you're canning, whether you live on a mountain peak or deep in a valley.

CHAPTER 6 storage, seals, and safety checks

YOUR CANNING EQUIPMENT IS CLEAN, DRY, AND BACK ON THE SHELVES WHERE IT BELONGS, and your well-sealed jars of pears and green beans are ready to store. If you do this job properly, many mouth-watering meals will await you.

STORAGE AREAS

"Cool," "dry," and "dark" are the key words when it comes to finding or setting up a storage area for your canned foods. Temperatures in that area should remain well below 95°F (35°C), but should never drop to freezing. High temperatures may destroy seals, will certainly destroy the vitamins in your food, and may very well cause food discoloration, too. Freezing temperatures may ruin the seals, but even when they don't, they'll reduce some canned foods to mush. High humidity can corrode the lids, breaking seals in the process, and daylight will cause discoloration.

An insulated but unheated basement, a dark pantry on an exterior wall of your home, a garage with closed cupboards and enough heat to prevent freezing will all work.

Arranging the Jars

One trick to arranging your jars of food is to place them so that you'll automatically grab for the jars that were canned first. If you processed batches of asparagus soup on June 1, June 15, and June 30, make sure the soup processed on June 1 is stored in front. This way, you won't eat all the newest soup first and be left with soup too old to keep.

Also make sure the jar labels are visible. If your shelves are below eye level, affix labels to the jar lids so that a downward glance will let you know when each jar was canned and what it contains. If your shelves are high, place the labels on the jars themselves and line up the jars with the labels facing outward. There's nothing quite as frustrating as having to pull out jar after jar in a dark storage area, trying to find the ones you want.

CHECKING SEALS

Your clean, colorful jars of peaches and pears, green beans, soup, chutney, salsa, and pickles are now lined up in neat rows. Your dinner guests are due to arrive in a hour, so you select a jar of curried zucchini soup, take it to the kitchen, and open it. Wrong! Let's try again. You select the jar, you take it to the kitchen, and you inspect the label, jar, and seal.

As you read the rest of this section, keep the following three rules in mind:

- Never taste food from a jar until you've inspected the jar carefully.
- Never taste food that looks or smells spoiled.
- Never taste food from a jar with an obviously broken seal.

Always check the date on the label first. As you get to know other home canners, you'll probably hear more than one of them boast about how many years their jars stayed well sealed. Turn a deaf ear or, better yet, give these folks a gentle lecture. Although it's true that good seals can sometimes last for years, you'll be doing yourself a favor if you force yourself to dispose of canned foods after one year of storage. If you haven't eaten the food by then, you probably processed too much in the first place, and there's no good reason to take chances with aged food.

Next, inspect the jar and lid. The lid should still be concave, liquid in the jar should cover the solid ingredients, and the headspace should be exactly what it was when you put the jar on the shelf. Look for the following signs of broken seals:

- The lid gives under pressure or is bulging. Even when bulging lids appear to be tightly sealed, don't eat the food. Air and the microorganisms in it have undoubtedly entered the jar.

- The jar looks dirty or molded. You washed and dried the jars before you stored them, so if their exteriors aren't clean now, chances are good that food has broken through the seal and spilled out. Mold on the outside of the jar may have invaded the contents, breaking the seal in the process.

- You smell something unpleasant. Nasty or unusual odors are a sure sign of food spoilage.

If you find any of these tell-tale signs, discard the contents and sterilize the jar following the instructions on the next page.

Next, turn the jar upside down and watch the contents. You may see a few air bubbles at first, but these should disappear very quickly. After the contents have settled, if you see very small air bubbles streaming from the rim back up through the ingredients, the seal has been broken and the food is unsafe to eat. Discard it and sterilize the jar.

Now open the jar, but don't taste the food yet. Look for the following signs:

- The contents spurt out when the lid is removed.

- Gas is expelled.

- Mold is evident on top of the food or on the underside of the lid.

- You notice an unusual odor.

- The food is slimy, or has an unusual texture.

The jar of food is unsafe to eat if any of the signs above is evident. Discard the contents and sterilize the jar.

Also look for cloudiness in the contents. This isn't always a clue that the food has spoiled. The starch in corn and dried beans can cause cloudiness, as can hard water, and impure or additive-laden salt. Fruit that is too ripe can cloud syrups, and fermented pickles can be cloudy without being spoiled, too.

If you notice cloudiness and also smell unusual odors, however, discard the food and sterilize the jar. If the cloudiness isn't accompanied by a bad smell, boil the food for 15 minutes before tasting it. (Traditionally, home canners have boiled low-acid foods for 15 minutes before tasting or eating them, even when the food looks fine. While this step isn't required, it's certainly an extra safety precaution that you may want to take.) If, while you boil or heat the food you notice any unusual odors, discard the food before tasting it.

Sometimes, the contents of a jar will change in appearance during storage, but these changes aren't dangerous. A list of examples follows:

- Cauliflower that is overmature when it's canned will often turn pink. When pickled, cauliflower can also react with vinegar in a similar fashion.

- Garlic in pickles will occasionally turn blue.

- When peeled tomatoes are allowed to sit for too long before processing, the pulp may separate from the liquid in the jar after processing. This enzymatic reaction isn't hazardous.

- Pears may turn pink due to their natural tannin content.

- Fruits, especially raw-packed ones, may very well float to the top of the jar. To prevent this from happening next time round, try switching to a lighter syrup or hot packing the pears.

DISCARDING FOOD AND STERILIZING JARS

Discarding the contents of suspect jars involves more than tossing them in the trash. If botulinum bacteria lurk in these ingredients, you need to make sure that no living creature has access to them. The safest ways to dispose of spoiled foods are to burn them or bury them in holes deep enough to hide them from animals (and people) fond of digging holes. Wash the contaminated jars thoroughly and boil them for 15 minutes before using them again.

Avoiding Food Spoilage

A friend of ours moved into a very old home recently and called us over to look at her basement shelves, which were covered with spoiled (we'd never seen such obvious signs of spoilage), home-canned foods. A quick glance confirmed several suspicions.

First, the lids on most of the jars were no longer sealed. On many, the screw bands hadn't been removed before the jars were stored in the damp basement. Rust had corroded the bands, which in turn had distorted the lids.

Second, the previous owner of the house had canned a great deal more food than he or she needed. Keeping track of how much of each recipe you put up every year can help you avoid this mistake.

Third, the home canner had never designed a storage system to help her avoid waste. The jars were all labeled with their content names, but none were dated. Some of the jars looked as if they were at least 30 years old.

CHAPTER 7 the recipes

FOR SOME FOOD LOVERS, culinary heaven is a crunchy dill pickle or crystal-clear jelly—a food that brings back memories of childhood snacks in grandma's kitchen. For others, it's a spicy hot salsa, lavishly spread over burritos, or a thick, rich chutney for an exotic curry. In selecting recipes for this book, we've taken into account as many different types of appetite as possible. You'll find flaming hot salsas, hearty soups, lusciously sweet fruit spreads, crisp pickles and relishes, savory sauces, fascinating chutney blends, and more. The only foods we've deliberately omitted are meat, poultry, and seafood. Although these can be safely canned at home, we believe that fruits and vegetables make tastier heat-processed products.

Our recipes are just a sampling, of course; hundreds of others are available today, and we encourage you to try them. Some canning-jar manufacturers carry wonderful booklets filled with tested recipes, and your local Cooperative Extension Service agent may also have recipes to share. If you're a computer user, by all means search the Net. The words "home canning," keyed into any search engine, will yield everything from online home-canning publications to recipes from canners around the world. Many Extension Services around the country also provide recipes online. Just one warning: When you're dealing with recipes from other home canners or older books, check the processing times and pressures against the information in the chart on pages 123–26.

For your browsing pleasure, we've divided our recipes into sections, each of which starts off with important information. "Jellies and Marmalades," for example, begins with an explanation of what makes a jelly jell and goes on to provide instructions for extracting the juice from which jellies are made. Take the time to read these introductory materials before you begin; they'll help make your first canning ventures successful.

One final word of advice: Relax! Sure, canning requires some caution, but once you've had some practice, you'll find that it's a thoroughly absorbing and enjoyable experience.

Reading Recipes

Each of our recipes contains an important list. Before you get started, take a look at the example below:

YIELD: **4 pints**

> Expect the recipe to yield enough to fill four one-pint jars. When making fruit spreads or foods that must be pressure canned, be sure to use the recommended jar size. Fruit spreads won't jell properly when they're packed in larger or smaller jars than those recommended, and pressure-canned foods may not be safely processed if you pack them in larger jars.

PACK: **Hot (or Raw)**

> This message let's you know in advance whether you'll be filling your jars with preheated or cold food. For hot-packed recipes, preheat the water in your canner to simmering. For raw-packed foods, preheat the canner water only until it's hot.

HEADSPACE: **½ inch**

> Leave the recommended amount of headspace when you pack your jars.

PROCESSING TIME: **5 minutes**

> The heading "Processing Time" indicates that the recipe must be processed in a boiling-water bath, not in a pressure canner. Remember to start timing only after the water in the canner has come to a rolling boil.

DIAL-GAUGE CANNER
TIME & PRESSURE: **45 minutes/11 pounds**

WEIGHTED-GAUGE CANNER
TIME & PRESSURE: **45 minutes/10 pounds**

> These two headings indicate that the food must be processed in either a dial-gauge pressure canner or a weighted-gauge pressure canner—not in a boiling-water bath! These time and pressure recommendations apply only to the size of jar recommended under the heading "Yield."

pickled vegetables and fruits

WHAT IS A PICKLE? We're all familiar with the famous kosher dill, but in canning terminology, the term "pickles" includes a number of preparations, from traditional fermented dill pickles and sauerkraut to "quick" pickles, relishes, chow-chows, chutneys, and piccalillis. All these foods share one common characteristic: high acidity levels, usually resulting from their vinegar content.

For the sake of convenience, we've divided our recipes for pickled products into two sections. In this one, you'll find basic information on pickling as well as recipes for quick-pickled fruits and vegetables. More exotic recipes for other pickled products can be found in the next sec-

tion. In neither section do we cover fermented pickled products—the ones our grandparents made by placing cucumbers, cabbage, or other vegetables in large crocks, covering them with brine, and allowing them to ferment for several weeks. We're skipping these foods for two reasons. First, the fermentation process can be difficult to master. Second, crisp fermented pickles and crunchy sauerkraut don't, in our opinion, can very well. By the time they've been heat processed, they're not quite as firm and delicious as we'd like. If you want to try your hand at making and processing these preparations, your local Cooperative Extension Service agent can provide safe instructions for doing so.

QUICK-PICKLED PRODUCTS

Quick pickled fruits and vegetables, which require no fermentation, are acidified with vinegar. The vegetables or fruits are either raw packed and covered with a boiling, vinegar-based syrup or are precooked and hot packed with this syrup. Some are first allowed to stand in a brine solution for a few hours or overnight and are then drained before raw packing or precooking.

Literally hundreds of delicious quick-pickle recipes exist, including recipes for whole cucumber dills, sweet bread-and-butter pickles, and "dilly beans" (dilled green beans).

PICKLING SAFETY GUIDELINES

If you're the type of cook who likes to add a dash of this or an extra cup of that, you'll need to quell some of your creativity when you work with pickled products. Changing the vinegar, food, and water proportions or using a vinegar of unknown acidity is dangerous. There's no harm in adding a few extra cloves of garlic, a dash of cayenne, or more sugar to a recipe, but please don't change the ratios between the main vegetable and/or fruit ingredients, the acidifying agents such as vinegar and citrus juice, and diluting agents such as water.

If you tamper with recipes at all (and we don't advise it), use the following rule of thumb: Every pint of pickles you prepare should include at least 1/4 cup of vinegar and/or other acidifiers just as strong in acid content. Avoid outdated pickle and relish recipes unless they meet this guideline. Unfortunately, botulinum thrives in pickles that aren't acid enough.

PICKLING INGREDIENTS

Vinegar plays a critical role in pickled products. Distilled white vinegar is often the best type for the job, although other commercial vinegars, including rice, wine, and cider vinegars, are also used. Cider vinegar tends to turn white vegetables brown, but we do enjoy its distinctive flavor. If color is important to you, just substitute an equal portion of distilled white vinegar.

Use only commercial vinegars, never homemade, as vinegar for pickling must be 50 to 60 grain strength (5% to 6% acetic acid). If you want to make a recipe less sour, add sugar to it but never decrease the amount of vinegar.

Neither chlorinated nor hard water makes good pickles. To soften hard tap water, boil it for 15 minutes and then let it stand for 24 hours. A film will appear on its upper surface, and sediment may rest at the bottom. Skim the scum off and ladle the water from the sediment. Then add 1 tablespoon of distilled white vinegar to each gallon of water before using it in your recipes.

To dechlorinate tap water, just leave a large, open container of it out overnight; the chlorine will dissipate. Bottled, distilled water also works well, but don't use mineral water, which is much too hard.

As in many home-canning recipes, whole fresh spices and herbs are usually preferable to the dried, ground versions, as the latter tend to darken heat-processed foods. In jars of pickled foods, the herbs and spices are often allowed to float freely. If you find these floating bits unattractive, just place the spices in a spice bag or stainless-steel spice ball when making the syrup. Don't forget to remove the bag or ball before packing the jars!

Food-grade alum is included in some older pickle recipes to help keep the pickles crisp. Today, pickling lime (or calcium hydroxide) produces the same effect in commercial pickles and is sometimes used as a soaking solution in home-canning recipes. We don't include lime in any of our recipes, however, because we don't believe it's necessary.

PICKLING EQUIPMENT AND UTENSILS

Preparing fresh-packed pickles doesn't require any specialized equipment, but acid ingredients such as vinegar will wreak havoc on utensils made of zinc, iron, brass, copper, or galvanized metal. Enameled, stainless steel, or glass saucepans, without cracks or chips, are best.

HEAT PROCESSING PICKLED FOODS

Quick-pickled products, when they're prepared with the correct proportion of vinegar, may always be processed in a boiling-water bath.

Quick-Pickling Problems and Causes

PROBLEM: Your cucumber pickles look great, but when you bite into them, they're hollow.

CAUSE: Sometimes, due to growing conditions, cucumbers are hollow when they're harvested.

PROBLEM: Your pickles look like bath-shrivelled thumbs.

CAUSE: Syrups in which salt, sugar, and vinegar are mixed in incorrect proportions can yield this effect, as can overcooking and overprocessing.

PROBLEM: Your pickles darken after processing.

CAUSE: Using dried spices or leaving whole spices in the brine will create this effect, as will using iron utensils, overcooking, or including hard water, cider vinegar, or iodized salt.

PROBLEM: Garlic turns blue after processing.

CAUSE: This is usually a result of using hard water.

PROBLEM: Your cucumber pickles are soggy.

CAUSE: Your cucumbers may have been harvested right after a heavy rain. We're serious! Waterlogged cucumbers won't make crisp pickles.

Sweet-and-Sour Baby Carrots

Freshly harvested immature carrots are best, but even the "baby" carrots sold in grocery stores will work. The latter aren't immature, of course. They're mature carrots that have been whittled down to an attractive size in a mechanical contraption similar to a rock polisher. Nevertheless, they're very tasty when prepared with the syrup described here.

YIELD: **4 half-pints**
PACK: **Hot**
HEADSPACE: **½ inch**
PROCESSING TIME: **15 minutes**

INGREDIENTS

   1 pound baby carrots
   1 cup distilled white vinegar
   1 cup water
   2 teaspoons salt
   ½ teaspoon crushed white peppercorns
   ¼ cup honey
   4 sprigs fresh dill
   4 baby onions or garlic cloves, peeled

METHOD

You needn't peel the carrots, but do wash them thoroughly and remove their green tops. In a saucepan, combine the vinegar, water, salt, and peppercorns. In a separate saucepan, bring 1 quart of water to a boil. Add the carrots to the boiling water and blanch them by boiling them for about 3 minutes.

As the carrots are blanching, bring the vinegar mixture to a boil. Simmer gently for a minute or two and then add the honey and return to a boil. Place a sprig of dill and a baby onion or garlic clove in each jar. Pack the hot carrots into jars and ladle the boiling syrup over them.

Pickled Hot Garlic

Garlic lovers will find themselves snacking on these delectable treats, but they're really meant to be used as flavorings for meats, seafood, and poultry. They also make tasty additions to salad dressings.

YIELD: **4 half-pints**
PACK: **Hot**
HEADSPACE: **1/2 inch**
PROCESSING TIME: **20 minutes**

INGREDIENTS

- 1 pound garlic cloves
- 4 sprigs fresh thyme
- 4 sprigs fresh rosemary
- 8 crushed white peppercorns
- 1 cup distilled white vinegar
- 1 cup dry white wine
- 1 long green chili pepper, seeded and chopped
- 3 tablespoons sugar
- 2 teaspoons salt

METHOD

Rather than peeling the garlic by crushing the cloves with the flat of a knife, cover them with boiling water for 10 seconds. Immediately drain and then cool the cloves by submerging them in ice water. The loosened skins will slip right off. Be sure to discard any bruised cloves.

Tie the thyme, rosemary, and crushed peppercorns in a muslin or cheesecloth bag. In a saucepan, combine the peeled garlic cloves and remaining ingredients. Then add the spice bag, bring to a boil, and boil for 5 minutes. Transfer the mixture, with the spice bag, to a large covered bowl and refrigerate it overnight.

The next day, return the mixture and spice bag to the saucepan and bring to a boil. Simmer for 5 minutes. Remove the spice bag, ladle the garlic cloves into jars, and cover with the hot liquid.

Recipe Tips

■ Remove the blossom end of each cucumber by slicing off and discarding 1/16 inch at the non-stem end. The enzymes in this portion make it prone to spoilage.

■ Remember to use canning or pickling salt rather than iodized table salt in all these recipes.

■ Wear rubber gloves when handling fresh hot peppers! And keep your hands away from your mouth! Removing the seeds, which are extremely hot, tones down fiery recipes.

Pickled Mushrooms

These delicious morsels make wonderful appetizers, but we do need to warn you that the recipe steps must be followed carefully, or the mushrooms won't absorb enough vinegar.

YIELD: **4 half-pints**
PACK: **Raw**
HEADSPACE: **1/2 inch**
PROCESSING TIME: **20 minutes**

INGREDIENTS

- ½ cup lemon juice
- ½ cup lime juice
- 6 cups trimmed mushrooms
- ½ cup distilled white vinegar
- ¼ cup balsamic vinegar
- 1 cup olive oil
- 1½ teaspoons salt
- ½ teaspoon oregano
- 4 crushed white peppercorns
- 4 bay leaves
- ¾ teaspoon dried basil
- 4 garlic cloves, peeled

METHOD

In a saucepan, bring the citrus juices to a boil. Add the mushrooms and return the liquid to a boil. Then turn down the heat and simmer for 5 minutes. Drain well.

In a large bowl, mix together the mushrooms and vinegars. Cover the bowl and allow the mushrooms to marinate for 12 hours. Then drain the mushrooms, reserving the vinegar marinade.

In a saucepan, combine the marinade, olive oil, salt, and spices, and bring the mixture to a boil. Place a clove of garlic in each jar and divide the marinated mushrooms among the jars as well. Then pour the boiling marinade over the mushrooms. (If you run short on liquid, add distilled white vinegar, not oil or water.)

German Pickled Vegetables

We find that the curry powder and mustard in this recipe add just the right amount of spiciness, but if you'd prefer hotter pickles, add one seeded red chili pepper to the vinegar syrup and remove it just before ladling the syrup over the packed vegetables.

YIELD: **5 pints**
PACK: **Hot**
HEADSPACE: **½ inch**
PROCESSING TIME: **15 minutes**

INGREDIENTS

- ½ cup salt
- 7 cups boiling water
- 2 pounds sliced pickling cucumbers
- 1½ pounds peeled, sliced onions
- 2 cups cauliflower florets
- 1 cup sliced carrots
- ¼ cup flour
- 1 cup honey
- 2 tablespoons mustard powder
- 1 tablespoon mustard seed
- 1 tablespoon celery seed
- 1 teaspoon curry powder
- 3 cups distilled white vinegar

METHOD

Dissolve the salt in the boiling water and allow the brine to cool. Place the sliced cucumbers in one bowl and the sliced onions in another. Pour half of the brine into each bowl. To hold the vegetables under the brine, place a large plate in each bowl and position two or three, clean water-filled jars on top of each plate. Allow the vegetables to soak overnight.

Place the cauliflower and carrots in a very large saucepan or stockpot, add water to cover, and bring to a boil. Cook for 3 to 4 minutes, then drain the vegetables and cool them in ice water right away. Drain again when cool.

Drain the cucumbers and onions, rinsing them several times to remove all excess salt. Then add them to the drained cauliflower and carrots.

In a small saucepan, combine the flour and spices. Slowly add the vinegar to these dry ingredients, then mix in the honey. Bring the mixture to a boil and cook for 5 minutes before removing from the heat.

Cover the vegetables with water and bring to a boil. Drain them immediately, return them to the stockpot, and add the thickened syrup. Return the mixture to a boil, then lower the heat and pack the jars.

Aunt Frank's Bread-and-Butter Pickles

Jars of these paper-thin delicacies make wonderful gifts— if you can hang on to them long enough to give any away.

YIELD: **4 pints**
PACK: **Hot**
HEADSPACE: **½ inch**
PROCESSING TIME: **10 minutes**

INGREDIENTS

- 1 gallon pickling cucumbers
- ½ cup salt
- Several cups cracked ice
- 5 cups sugar
- 1½ teaspoons turmeric
- 2 tablespoons white mustard seed
- 1 teaspoon celery seed
- 5 cups cider vinegar

METHOD

Wash the cucumbers thoroughly and cut into paper-thin slices. In a large bowl, mix the slices and salt, then cover with ice cubes. Place a large plate on top of the ice and weigh it down with two or three clean, water-filled jars. Allow the salted slices to stand for 3 hours.

Drain the slices thoroughly and place them in a large saucepan. In a mixing bowl, combine the sugar and turmeric. Then add the remaining spices and the vinegar. Pour this mixture over the cucumber slices and heat slowly. Be careful not to let the syrup come to a boil. Ladle the hot cucumbers and syrup into jars.

Pickled Cocktail Onions

These tiny onions taste unbelievably good—too good to waste in Gibsons! Try serving them straight, but be sure to provide an ample supply of toothpicks, too, or the onions will disappear by the handful.

YIELD: **4 pints**
PACK: **Raw**
HEADSPACE: **½ inch**
PROCESSING TIME: **10 minutes**

INGREDIENTS

- 2 quarts peeled pearl onions
- ¾ cup salt
- 1 quart water
- 1 quart white wine vinegar
- ¾ cup sugar
- 3 tablespoons mixed pickling spices
- 1 tablespoon peeled, grated horseradish
- 1 small red chili pepper, seeded

METHOD

Place the onions in a large bowl. Mix the salt and water, then pour this brine over the onions. Place a large plate on top of the onions and weigh the plate down with clean, water-filled jars to keep the onions submerged in the brine. After 24 hours, drain and rinse the onions several times to remove the excess salt.

Combine the vinegar and sugar in a large saucepan. Tie the mixed pickling spices and horseradish in a muslin or cheesecloth bag. Add the bag to the mixture along with the whole, seeded chili pepper. Simmer the mixture for 15 minutes. Pack the onions into jars and return the syrup to a boil. Remove the spice bag and chili pepper before ladling the boiling syrup over the onions.

Mixed Pickling Spices

Many recipes call for a premixed combination of spices known as mixed pickling spices. You'll find this product in the canning or spice section of your supermarket. If you'd like to prepare your own, just combine the following ingredients:

- 1 cinnamon stick, broken into pieces
- 1 dried chili pepper, broken into pieces
- 2 teaspoons ginger
- 1-1/2 tablespoons crushed bay leaves
- 1 tablespoon cardamom seed
- 1-1/2 tablespoons mustard seed
- 1 tablespoon allspice
- 1 tablespoon coriander
- Whole peppercorns to taste

Classic-But-Quick Dill Pickles

We're absolutely convinced that homely dill pickles—chilled, crunchy, and swimming in spiced vinegar—
are gifts straight from heaven. No refrigerator should lack a jar of them.

YIELD: **7 pints**
PACK: **Raw**
HEADSPACE: **½ inch**
PROCESSING TIME: **20 minutes**

INGREDIENTS

  8 pounds pickling cucumbers

1½ cups salt

  2 gallons water

1½ quarts distilled white vinegar

  ¼ cup sugar

  2 quarts water

  3 tablespoons mustard seed

  2 tablespoons mixed pickling spices

14 sprigs fresh dill

  7 tablespoons dill seed

21 whole black peppercorns

METHOD

Remove a ¹⁄₁₆-inch-thick slice from the blossom end of each cucumber, but leave the stems attached. Place the cucumbers in a large stockpot. Dissolve ¾ cup of the salt in 2 gallons of water. Pour this brine over the cucumbers and allow them to stand for 24 hours. Drain well, rinsing several times to remove all excess salt.

In a large stockpot, combine the vinegar, remaining salt, sugar, 2 quarts of water, and mustard seed. Tie the mixed pickling spices in a muslin or cheesecloth bag and add the bag to the mixture. Bring the mixture to a boil.

Place 2 sprigs of fresh dill in each canning jar. Pack the jars with cucumbers, and to each jar, add 1 tablespoon of dill seed and 3 black peppercorns. Remove the spice bag and cover the cucumbers with boiling syrup.

Low-Sodium Sweet-and-Sour Dills

If you're on a low-sodium diet, don't despair! Flavorful pickles can still be yours.
When we first tasted these hearty sliced pickles, we couldn't believe they contained so little salt.
If you need to watch your sugar intake, too, just reduce the sugar in the recipe.

YIELD: **7 pints**
PACK: **Raw**
HEADSPACE: **½ inch**
PROCESSING TIME: **10 minutes**

INGREDIENTS

  4 pounds pickling cucumbers

  6 cups distilled white vinegar

  6 cups sugar

  1 tablespoon salt

  1 tablespoon celery seed

  2 teaspoons mustard seed

  ½ teaspoon cayenne pepper (optional)

  2 large onions, peeled and sliced

14 sprigs fresh dill

METHOD

Remove about ¹⁄₁₆ inch from the blossom end of each cucumber. Then slice the cucumbers into quarters along their lengths. In a large saucepan, combine the vinegar, sugar, salt, celery seed, mustard seed, and optional cayenne pepper. Bring the mixture to a boil.

Place several onion slices and 2 sprigs of fresh dill in each jar. Pack the cucumbers into the jars and cover them with the boiling syrup.

Patti's Dilly Beans

*Decades ago, dilled green beans—
pencil thin, tender, and tart—were
a staple in many American
pantries. They're once again
becoming popular, so we thought
we'd share the best dilly-bean
recipe we've ever run into.*

YIELD: **4 pints**
PACK: **Raw**
HEADSPACE: **½ inch**
PROCESSING TIME: **10 minutes**

INGREDIENTS

    2 pounds green snap or
       yellow beans
    2 cups water
    2 cups distilled white vinegar
    3 tablespoons salt
    4 sprigs fresh dill
    4 garlic cloves, peeled
    4 teaspoons red pepper flakes

METHOD

Snap the stems from the beans.
Then cut the beans into 1- or 2-
inch lengths. (For especially pretty
finished jars, measure the height of
your jars and cut each bean ¾ inch
shorter so that you can fill the jars
by packing the beans vertically
or diagonally.)

Combine the water, vinegar, and
salt in a saucepan and bring the
mixture to a boil. Place 1 sprig of
dill, 1 garlic clove, and 1 teaspoon
of red pepper flakes in each jar.
Pack the beans into the jars and
ladle the boiling vinegar mixture
over them.

Japanese Pickled Radish

*Crunchy, mildly sweet daikon
radishes are now fairly common in
most grocery stores, so you should
have no trouble preparing this
delectable condiment.*

YIELD: **4 pints**
PACK: **Raw**
HEADSPACE: **½ inch**
PROCESSING TIME: **10 minutes**

INGREDIENTS

    2   pounds daikon radishes
    2½ cups rice wine vinegar
    1   cup water
    2   tablespoons sugar
    1   tablespoon peeled, minced
        gingerroot
    4   garlic cloves, peeled and
        minced
    1   hot chili pepper (optional)
    2   teaspoons salt

METHOD

After thoroughly washing the
radishes, peel them and cut the
flesh into thin slivers. In a large
saucepan, combine the remaining
ingredients and bring the mixture
to a boil.

Pack the radish slivers into jars.
Remove the hot pepper from the
boiling syrup and ladle the syrup
over the radishes.

Catherine's Pickled Hot Peppers

*These bite-sized treats make
superb snacks, garnishes, or
appetizing tidbits for salad dressings and sauces. Be sure to choose
red, yellow, and green varieties for
the best presentation.*

YIELD: **8 pints**
PACK: **Raw**
HEADSPACE: **½ inch**
PROCESSING TIME: **15 minutes**

INGREDIENTS

    4 quarts mixed hot peppers
    4 cups distilled white vinegar
    4 cups water
    8 garlic cloves, peeled
    8 sprigs fresh dill
    4 teaspoons salt

METHOD

If the peppers are very small, leave
them whole. If they're large, seed
them and chop them into bite-
sized pieces. In a large saucepan,
combine the vinegar and water
and bring to a boil. Turn the heat
down to a simmer.

Place a clove of garlic and a sprig of
dill in each jar. Pack the peppers into
the jars and sprinkle the salt over
them. Cover with the simmering
vinegar mixture.

Susie Gray's Sweet Pickle Chunks

Chilled and served as a side dish, these Kentucky pickles will prove irresistible with almost any meal.

YIELD: **7 pints**
PACK: **Raw**
HEADSPACE: **½ inch**
PROCESSING TIME: **10 minutes**

INGREDIENTS

1 gallon pickling cucumbers
3¾ cups distilled white vinegar
3 cups sugar
3 tablespoons salt
4½ teaspoons celery seed
4½ teaspoons turmeric
¾ teaspoon mustard seed

METHOD

After washing the cucumbers, place them in a large stockpot and cover them with boiling water. Allow them to stand for 4 to 5 hours. Then drain them well and cut into chunks.

Combine the remaining ingredients in a large saucepan and bring to a boil. Pack the cucumber chunks into clean jars and cover with the boiling syrup.

Aunt Pearl's Bread-and-Butter Pickles

The recipe for these exceptional sweet-and-sour pickles was given to us by our friend, Cindy Wheeler, who says it's the most popular recipe in her canning collection.

YIELD: **4 pints**
PACK: **Hot**
HEADSPACE: **½ inch**
PROCESSING TIME: **15 minutes**

INGREDIENTS

8 cups thinly sliced pickling cucumbers
2 cups thinly sliced onions
½ cup salt
4 green peppers, seeded and diced
2 cups cider vinegar
4 teaspoons salt
3 cups sugar
2 teaspoons celery seed
2 teaspoons turmeric
1 cinnamon stick

METHOD

In a large mixing bowl, combine the cucumber and onion slices. Sprinkle with ½ cup of salt and let stand for one hour.

Drain the liquid from the cucumbers and onions and combine them with the remaining ingredients in a large saucepan. Bring to a boil and cook for 30 minutes. Pack the pickles into jars. Remove the cinnamon stick from the syrup and ladle over the pickles.

Pickled Asparagus Tips

A truly special gift, pickled asparagus tips are a rarity, even in gourmet food shops. Reserve the tougher stems and use them in the asparagus soup recipe on page 96.

YIELD: **4 pints**
PACK: **Raw**
HEADSPACE: **½ inch**
PROCESSING TIME: **15 minutes**

INGREDIENTS

3 cups white wine vinegar
3 cups water
2 teaspoons salt
1 tablespoon mixed pickling spices
4 crushed black peppercorns
1 crushed bay leaf
3 tablespoons honey
4 pounds asparagus tips

METHOD

In a saucepan, combine the vinegar, water, and salt. Tie the mixed pickling spices, peppercorns, and bay leaf in a muslin or cheesecloth bag and add the bag to the mixture. Bring the mixture to a boil, turn down the heat, and simmer for 10 minutes. Then add the honey and simmer for another 5 minutes.

As the syrup is simmering, cut the asparagus tips 1 inch shorter than the height of the pint jars. Pack the asparagus into the jars and cover with the hot syrup. Discard the spice bag.

Georgia's Pickled Green Tomatoes

With this recipe, Georgia Shuford proved to us that harvesting a late summer garden full of green tomatoes can be an uplifting experience.

YIELD: **7 pints**

PACK: **Hot**

HEADSPACE: **½ inch**

PROCESSING TIME: **10 minutes**

INGREDIENTS

- 1 gallon green tomatoes, cored and cut into chunks
- 1½ quarts peeled, sliced onions
- ½ cup salt
- 2 cups brown sugar
- 2 teaspoons mixed pickling spices
- 2 quarts distilled white vinegar
- ½ quart water
- ½ teaspoon turmeric

METHOD

In a large mixing bowl, combine the tomatoes, onions, and salt. Allow the mixture to stand overnight, then drain the liquid from the vegetables.

In a large stockpot, mix together the brown sugar, mixed pickling spices, vinegar, water, and turmeric. Bring to a boil, then add the drained vegetables. Return the mixture to a boil. Pack the jars and add enough liquid to cover the vegetables completely.

Pickled Ginger

If you frequent Japanese restaurants, you may already be addicted to this spicy treat, which is often served in small, shallow dishes. The thin slices also make a fine relish on cold roast-beef sandwiches.

YIELD: **4 half-pints**

PACK: **Hot**

HEADSPACE: **½ inch**

PROCESSING TIME: **10 minutes**

INGREDIENTS

- Peeled gingerroot (see "Method")
- 2 cups rice vinegar
- 1 cup distilled white vinegar
- 1 tablespoon sugar
- 3 tablespoons soy sauce or miso

METHOD

Cut the peeled ginger, along the grain, into paper-thin slices, measuring out 3 cups. Then place the slices in a bowl filled with ice water. Cover the bowl and refrigerate for 8 to 10 hours.

Drain the ginger and combine it with the remaining ingredients in a small saucepan. Bring to a boil. Ladle the ginger and liquid into jars.

Sweet Pickled Pears

Firmer pear varieties are best for this recipe, as precooking will soften them considerably. We recommend Seckel or Bartlett. Of course, if your pears do soften too much during processing, just use this recipe as a relish or sauce! It's delicious with both meat and fish.

YIELD: **6 pints**

PACK: **Hot**

HEADSPACE: **½ inch**

PROCESSING TIME: **15 minutes**

INGREDIENTS

- 1 cup sugar
- 2½ cups water
- 1½ cups distilled white vinegar
- 1 lemon, thinly sliced
- 2 tablespoons mixed pickling spices
- 1 cinnamon stick, broken into pieces
- 2 teaspoons whole cloves
- 6 allspice berries
- 2 thin slices peeled gingerroot
- 12 pounds pears, peeled, cored, and halved
- ½ cup honey

METHOD

In a large saucepan, combine the sugar, water, vinegar, and lemon slices. Tie the spices and ginger in a muslin or cheesecloth bag and add the bag to the mixture. Bring to a boil, turn down the heat, and simmer for 5 minutes.

Add to the simmering syrup as many pear halves as will fit in one layer and simmer over low heat for about 10 minutes or until barely tender. Remove these halves and add another batch. Repeat until all the pears have been simmered. Then add the honey to the syrup, return to a boil, and simmer for 5 minutes. Remove the spice bag from the syrup, pack the pears into jars, and cover with the syrup.

Sweet-and-Sour Peaches

Serve these pickled peaches with roast meats. They're extremely flavorful, so don't overdo the portions.

YIELD: **7 pints**
PACK: **Hot**
HEADSPACE: ½ **inch**
PROCESSING TIME: **10 minutes**

INGREDIENTS

- 2 cups white grape juice
- 1 quart cider vinegar
- ½ cup sugar
- 2 tablespoons grated lemon peel
- 4 allspice berries
- 15 whole cloves
- 3 cinnamon sticks, broken into pieces
- 1 tablespoon minced, crystallized ginger
- 10 pounds peeled, pitted, and quartered peaches

METHOD

Combine the grape juice, vinegar, sugar, and lemon peel in a large saucepan. Tie the whole spices and ginger in a muslin or cheesecloth bag and add the bag to the mixture. Bring to a boil, simmer for 5 minutes, then add the peach halves. Return to a boil, lower the heat, and simmer for another 5 minutes. Ladle the peaches and syrup into the jars. Discard the spice bag.

Southern Watermelon-Rind Pickles

You don't need to be from Dixie to enjoy these pickles or the visions they bring to mind: sultry summer days, picnic tables under moss-laden oaks, fine food, and the company of close friends.

YIELD: **4 pints**
PACK: **Hot**
HEADSPACE: ½ **inch**
PROCESSING TIME: **10 minutes**

INGREDIENTS

- Rind of one large watermelon
- ¾ cup salt
- 5 cups cold water
- 2 cups distilled white vinegar
- 2 cups water
- 2 cups sugar
- 6 teaspoons whole cloves
- 6 allspice berries
- 1 cup honey

METHOD

To prepare the rind, first trim away the dark skin from the outside and any remnants of melon from the inside. Then cut the rind into bite-sized pieces. Measure out 8 cups of these pieces and place them in a very large bowl. Mix the salt and 5 cups of cold water, then pour this brine over the pieces of rind to cover them. Allow the rind to stand overnight.

Rinse and drain the rind several times to remove all excess salt. Place the pieces in a large stockpot, add water to cover, and bring the water to a boil. Turn down the heat and simmer very gently for 5 minutes. Drain the pieces of rind well and place them in a clean mixing bowl.

In a saucepan, combine the vinegar, 2 cups of water, and sugar. Tie the cloves and allspice in a muslin or cheesecloth bag and place the bag in the mixture. Bring the mixture to a boil, turn down the heat, and simmer for 10 minutes. Pour the hot syrup over the pieces of rind, cover the bowl, and allow the rind to stand overnight. (Place the spice bag in the bowl, too.)

On the following day, bring the rind, syrup, honey, and spice bag to a boil, turn down the heat, and simmer for about 5 minutes or until the rind is slightly translucent. Be careful, as overcooking will turn the morsels to mush! Remove the spice bag before ladling into jars.

Cinnamon Apple Rings

Apple rings look best when they're stacked in their jars, so be sure to have wide-mouth jars on hand. If you only have access to standard jars, simply slice the apples into quarters or chunks, instead.

YIELD: **4 pints**
PACK: **Raw**
HEADSPACE: **½ inch**
PROCESSING TIME: **10 minutes**

INGREDIENTS

8 pounds tart green apples
1 cup distilled white vinegar
1 cup cider vinegar
5 cups sugar
2 tablespoons grated lemon peel
3 cinnamon sticks, broken into pieces
6 allspice berries
15 whole cloves

METHOD

In order to slice the apples into rings, you'll need to peel and core them without cutting the fruit apart. An apple peeler-and-corer comes in handy here, but cutting out the cores with a long slender knife will work. After you've removed the cores, slice the apples into ¼-inch-thick rings.

Combine the two vinegars and sugar in a saucepan. Tie the spices and grated lemon peel in a muslin or cheesecloth bag and add the bag to the mixture. Bring to a boil, turn down the heat, and simmer gently for 15 minutes.

As the syrup is simmering, stack the apple rings neatly in wide-mouth jars. Remove the spice bag from the simmering syrup and ladle the syrup over the apples.

Pickled Lemon Slices

As a condiment with Indian or Caribbean food, pickled lemons are simply glorious. Tart, but not overwhelmingly so, their flavor tends to bring out the nuances of foods they accompany.

YIELD: **6 half-pints**
PACK: **Hot**
HEADSPACE: **½ inch**
PROCESSING TIME: **10 minutes**

INGREDIENTS

1½ quarts distilled white vinegar
½ cup salt
2 tablespoons sugar
15 whole cloves
1 teaspoon nutmeg
1 teaspoon mace
1 tablespoon mustard seed
1 hot chili pepper, seeded
15 lemons
6 garlic cloves, peeled (optional)

METHOD

In a large saucepan, combine the vinegar, salt, and sugar. Tie the cloves in a muslin or cheesecloth bag and add it to the mixture, along with the nutmeg, mace, mustard seed, and chili pepper. Bring to a boil, lower the heat, and simmer for 15 minutes.

While the syrup is simmering, cut the lemons into thin slices. Add the slices to the syrup and simmer for about 10 minutes or until the lemons are tender.

Place one whole garlic clove in each jar. Remove the spice bag and whole pepper from the syrup. Ladle the lemons into the jars and cover with simmering syrup.

Spiced Cherry Pickles

These are terrific straight from the jar, but they also make a very tasty condiment for roast meats.

YIELD: **4 pints**
PACK: **Hot**
HEADSPACE: **½ inch**
PROCESSING TIME: **10 minutes**

INGREDIENTS

10 cups pitted, fresh sweet cherries
½ cup lemon juice
1 cinnamon stick, broken into pieces
12 whole cloves
4 allspice berries
3 thin slices peeled ginger-root
2½ cups distilled white vinegar
¾ cup sugar

METHOD

In a large bowl, mix the cherries and 2 tablespoons of the lemon juice. Cover and refrigerate for 4 hours.

Tie the cinnamon-stick pieces, cloves, allspice, and ginger in a muslin or cheesecloth bag. Place the bag in a large saucepan, along with the remaining lemon juice, the vinegar, and the sugar. Bring to a boil, lower the heat, and simmer for 15 minutes. Drain the cherries well, add them to the simmering syrup, and return to a boil. Remove the spice bag before ladling into jars.

the **7**
recipes

relishes, chow-chows, chutneys, and piccalillis

AS A CLASS OF FOODS, relishes may seem to lack romance. After all, they're basically just diced pickles, right? While we can't argue that relishes aren't diced pickles (that's exactly what they are), we can make a great case for relishes as gourmet foods. First, no two relishes taste alike. Their range of flavors is astounding. Second, the foods they complement, from hot dogs to cold cuts and from curries to crusty breads, are virtually limitless. And finally, many relishes are downright exotic.

Let's take chutneys as an example. Indulging in one of these sweet-and-sour Indian relishes is like taking an affordable vacation. Close your eyes, take one taste, and you're dining on delicious curries, deep in the heart of the tropics. No heavy suitcases, airport fiascos, or bad hotels; just fine food and flights of fancy.

Traditionally, chutneys are used as condiments on curries. Their fruity flavors take the sting from hot foods, and their sweetness complements savory flavors. Today's gourmet diners, however, enjoy chutneys with fish, cold meats, and casseroles as well, and even eat them as jams on bread.

Piccalillis, although they're now common in North America, were probably developed from chutney recipes brought to this continent by sea-faring voyagers returning from India. Early recipes often bear titles such as India Relish.

Legend has it that chow-chow (another type of mixed-vegetable relish) was invented by Napoleon's chef, who is said to have carried his recipe to London—and to the famous makers of preserves, Crosse & Blackwell—when Napoleon left for St. Helena. The actual history of chow-chows is vague, but like piccalillis, they were probably imitations of oriental relishes; their spice combinations are often distinctly Indian.

In this section, we offer a sampling of a wide range of relishes. They're all pickled products (they're acidified with significant amounts of vinegar) and can all be processed in a boiling-water bath. Be sure to follow the safety guidelines on page 61 when preparing and processing these foods.

Recipe Tips

■ Use only canning or pickling salt in these recipes.

■ Use nonreactive saucepans, stockpots, bowls, and utensils when making these high-acid recipes.

■ Remember to chop or dice vegetables and fruits into pieces of equal size so that the ingredients will be heat processed evenly throughout.

■ Cook chutneys slowly in an uncovered saucepan so that excess liquid in the ingredients will evaporate, leaving you with a smooth-textured and nearly jamlike sauce. To test a cooked chutney, run a wooden spoon across its surface. If the spoon leaves a path that doesn't fill up with liquid right away, your chutney is thoroughly cooked.

Extraordinary Hot Dog Relish

What would the world of relishes be without baseball stands, hot dogs, and our much-loved national favorite—crunchy, mustard-colored hot dog relish.

YIELD: **4 pints**
PACK: **Hot**
HEADSPACE: **¼ inch**
PROCESSING TIME: **15 minutes**

INGREDIENTS

    5 cups peeled, cored, and diced tomatoes

    3 red bell peppers, seeded and diced

    3 sweet green peppers, seeded and diced

    2 cups diced cucumbers

    2 cups peeled, diced onions

    ¼ cup salt

    ¼ cup flour

    1 cup granulated sugar

  1½ cups packed brown sugar

    3 teaspoons turmeric

    1 cup water

    1 tablespoon prepared mustard

    1 tablespoon mustard seed

    2 cups distilled white vinegar

METHOD

Mix the tomatoes, peppers, cucumbers, onions, and salt in a large bowl. Cover the bowl and let stand overnight. Rinse and drain well to remove all excess salt.

In a large saucepan, combine the flour, sugar, and turmeric. Slowly stir in the water. Then add the mustard, mustard seed, and vinegar. Bring to a boil, lower the heat, and simmer for 10 minutes. Add the tomatoes and vegetables and return the mixture to a boil. Reduce the heat again and simmer for about 30 minutes or until the relish has thickened. Ladle into jars.

Norma Jean's Pepper Relish

One of the easiest-to-make but most delicious relishes we've ever had the privilege of tasting, Norma Jean's colorful condiment is pleasingly tasty and mild.

YIELD: **5 pints**
PACK: **Hot**
HEADSPACE: **¼ inch**
PROCESSING TIME: **10 minutes**

INGREDIENTS

    6 sweet green peppers, seeded

    6 red bell peppers, seeded

    6 onions, peeled

    2 cups distilled white vinegar

    1 tablespoon salt

    2 cups sugar

METHOD

Grind or finely chop the peppers and onions, then place them in a large bowl. Cover with boiling water and let stand for 10 minutes. Drain well.

Combine all the ingredients in a large saucepan and boil for 10 minutes before ladling into jars.

Barbara's Red-and-Green Relish

Here's a classic green-tomato relish—chunky, tasty, and straight from the summer garden.

YIELD: **7 pints**
PACK: **Hot**
HEADSPACE: **¼ inch**
PROCESSING TIME: **10 minutes**

INGREDIENTS

    1 quart cored, diced green tomatoes

    1 quart peeled, cored, and diced ripe tomatoes

    5 onions, peeled and diced

    ¼ cup salt

    3 red bell peppers, seeded and diced

    2 sweet green peppers, seeded and diced

    2 cups distilled white vinegar

    2 cups sugar

    ¼ cup mustard seed (optional)

METHOD

Place the tomatoes and onions in a bowl, sprinkle with the salt, and allow to stand overnight. Then drain well, pressing out the brine. Combine all the ingredients in a large saucepan and bring to a boil. Lower the heat and simmer for 30 minutes before ladling into jars.

Clara's Zucchini Relish

If you've overplanted zucchini in your backyard garden, Clara's delicious relish will save the day. No midsummer searches for friends to haul the extra harvest away!

INGREDIENTS

    10 cups diced zucchini
     4 cups diced carrots
     4 cups peeled, diced onions
     5 tablespoons salt
     2 red bell peppers, seeded
        and diced
     2 sweet green peppers,
        seeded and diced
     1 tablespoon celery seed
     1 tablespoon turmeric
    2¼ cups cider vinegar
     4 cups sugar

YIELD: **8 pints**
PACK: **Hot**
HEADSPACE: **½ inch**
PROCESSING TIME: **10 minutes**

METHOD

In a large bowl, mix the zucchini, carrots, onions, and salt. Allow these ingredients to stand overnight, then rinse and drain them thoroughly. Combine all the ingredients in a large saucepan and bring to a boil. Boil for 15 minutes before ladling into jars.

Cranberry-Orange Relish

This relish is superb on turkey, of course, but don't limit your enjoyment to Thanksgiving day. With chicken salads and sandwiches, this colorful condiment is scrumptious.

YIELD: **6 half-pints**
PACK: **Hot**
HEADSPACE: **¼ inch**
PROCESSING TIME: **15 minutes**

INGREDIENTS

     1 cinnamon stick, broken
        into pieces
     6 allspice berries
    12 whole cloves
     3 oranges, peeled, seeded,
        and diced
     3 cups minced fresh
        cranberries
     1 cup cranapple juice
     ½ cup golden raisins
     ½ cup peeled, diced onion
     1 teaspoon salt
     1 cup packed brown sugar
     1 cup cider vinegar
     2 tablespoons Grand Marnier

METHOD

Tie the cinnamon-stick pieces, allspice, and cloves in a muslin or cheesecloth bag. Combine the remaining ingredients in a large saucepan and add the spice bag to them. Bring to a boil, turn down the heat, and simmer, covered, for 15 minutes. Then cook uncovered for another 15 minutes or until the relish thickens. Remove the spice bag before ladling into jars.

Jicama-Carrot Relish

A relatively mild relish, we recommend this one for seafood, as its subtle flavors won't disguise the delicate flavors of fine fish.

YIELD: **6 half-pints**
PACK: **Hot**
HEADSPACE: **¼ inch**
PROCESSING TIME: **15 minutes**

INGREDIENTS

     3 cups peeled, cubed jicama
     2 cups diced carrots
     ½ cup peeled, diced onion
     1 tablespoon seeded, diced
        jalapeño pepper (optional)
     6 tablespoons peeled, minced
        gingerroot
     6 garlic cloves, peeled and
        minced
     ½ cup lemon juice
     ½ cup distilled white vinegar
     2 tablespoons brown sugar
     1 teaspoon salt

METHOD

Combine all the ingredients in a large saucepan and bring to a boil. Turn down the heat and simmer for about 30 minutes or until slightly thickened. Ladle into jars.

Spicy Plum Relish

*A spicier version of an old Swiss recipe,
this relish is best served, either hot or cold,
as a side dish with meat and poultry meals.
The recipe takes three days to make,
but it's worth every moment.*

YIELD: **6 pints**

PACK: **Hot**

HEADSPACE: **½ inch**

PROCESSING TIME: **10 minutes**

INGREDIENTS

- 2½ cups red wine
- 2½ cups cider vinegar
- 4 cups sugar
- 18 whole cloves
- 3 cinnamon sticks, broken into pieces
- 1 tablespoon peeled, minced horseradish
- 1 tablespoon peeled, minced gingerroot
- 5 pounds plums

METHOD

Combine the wine, vinegar, and sugar in a large saucepan. Tie the cloves, cinnamon-stick pieces, horseradish, and ginger in a muslin or cheesecloth bag and add the bag to the mixture. Bring to a boil, lower the heat, and simmer for 20 minutes. Remove the pan from the heat and discard the spice bag.

Prick the skins of the plums and place them in a large bowl. When the syrup has cooled, pour it over the plums and let stand at room temperature for 10 to 12 hours.

Drain the syrup from the plums, return the syrup to a boil, and allow it to cool again. Then pour the cool syrup over the plums and let stand for another night.

On the third day, place the plums and syrup in a large saucepan and cook over very low heat, removing the pan from the heat as soon as the skins of the plums begin to break and the plums are thoroughly heated. Do not allow the syrup to boil. Ladle the plums into jars. Return the syrup to a boil and cook over high heat until thick before ladling over the plums.

Horseradish Relish

Many years ago, the father of one of the authors used to celebrate every mouthful of this fiery condiment by dancing around the dining-room table, fanning his mouth. His children adored these performances and slowly learned to love horseradish, too.

YIELD: **5 pints**

PACK: **Hot**

HEADSPACE: **½ inch**

PROCESSING TIME: **10 minutes**

INGREDIENTS

- 5 pounds peeled, cored, and diced tomatoes
- 1 cinnamon stick, broken into pieces
- 4 allspice berries
- 4 whole cloves
- 4 red bell peppers, seeded and diced
- 4 onions, peeled and diced
- ½ pound peeled, minced horseradish
- 1½ cups packed brown sugar
- 1¾ cups cider vinegar
- 2 tablespoons salt
- 3 tablespoons mustard seed
- 2 tablespoons dill seed

METHOD

Place the diced tomatoes in a plastic sieve and allow them to drain for 3 hours. Tie the cinnamon-stick pieces, allspice berries, and cloves in a muslin or cheesecloth bag. Combine the remaining ingredients in a large saucepan. Then add the tomatoes and the spice bag.

Bring the mixture to a boil, lower the heat, and simmer, stirring frequently, for 45 minutes. Remove the spice bag and ladle the relish into jars.

Papaya-Cucumber Relish

You wouldn't think that papayas—so mild in flavor—could add as much flavor to a relish, but this recipe will convince you otherwise.

YIELD: **6 half-pints**
PACK: **Hot**
HEADSPACE: **½ inch**
PROCESSING TIME: **15 minutes**

INGREDIENTS

½ cup peeled, diced onion

2 tablespoons minced fresh mint

2 cups distilled white vinegar

2 tablespoons sugar

1 teaspoon salt

1 tablespoon honey

3 cups peeled, seeded, and diced papaya

3 cups peeled, diced cucumbers

METHOD

In a large saucepan, combine the onion, mint, vinegar, sugar, and salt. Bring to a boil and simmer for 10 minutes. Add the honey, papaya, and cucumber, and continue to simmer until the cucumbers start to soften. Then ladle into jars.

Chili-Corn Relish

This colorful, sugarless relish may be a bit too hot for some folks. To make it milder, just reduce the number of chilis or eliminate them entirely and add one more sweet pepper, instead.

YIELD: **7 half-pints**
PACK: **Hot**
HEADSPACE: **½ inch**
PROCESSING TIME: **20 minutes**

INGREDIENTS

5 cups corn kernels, fresh or frozen

1 cup finely chopped cabbage

2 onions, peeled and diced

1 sweet green pepper, seeded and diced

1 red bell pepper, seeded and diced

2 green chili peppers, seeded and diced

2½ cups distilled white vinegar

1 cup apple juice

1 tablespoon salt

1 tablespoon celery seed

1 tablespoon mustard seed

METHOD

Bring all the ingredients to a boil in a large saucepan. Turn down the heat and simmer, stirring frequently, for 45 minutes or until the relish thickens. Ladle into jars immediately.

Green Tomato Chutney

Tart, sweet, and spicy, this chutney has a pretty ferocious bite! We recommend it highly for red-pepper lovers.

YIELD: **6 half-pints**
PACK: **Hot**
HEADSPACE: **½ inch**
PROCESSING TIME: **10 minutes**

INGREDIENTS

- 4 dried hot red peppers
- 2 pounds cored, chopped green tomatoes
- ½ pound peeled, cored, and chopped green apples
- ½ pound peeled, chopped onion
- ½ cup raisins
- ¾ cup packed brown sugar
- 1 tablespoon peeled, minced gingerroot
- 4 garlic cloves, peeled and minced
- 1½ cups cider vinegar
- 2 tablespoons lemon juice

METHOD

Break the dried hot peppers into pieces and discard the seeds. Combine all the ingredients in a large saucepan, bring to a boil, and simmer slowly, stirring frequently, for 1 hour or until the chutney thickens. Ladle into jars.

Sugarless Tomato Chutney

There's no reason why chutneys need to include sugar. Apple juice and grape juice work well as thickeners and provide their own wonderful flavors, too.

YIELD: **8 half-pints**
PACK: **Hot**
HEADSPACE: **½ inch**
PROCESSING TIME: **20 minutes**

INGREDIENTS

- ½ cup apple juice
- ¾ cup white grape juice
- 5 cups peeled, cored, and chopped tomatoes
- 4 onions, peeled and chopped
- 1 sweet green pepper, seeded and chopped
- 1 dried hot red pepper
- 4 tart green apples, peeled, cored, and chopped
- 1 cup golden raisins
- 1¼ cups cider vinegar
- 2 teaspoons salt
- 2 teaspoons curry powder
- ½ teaspoon cloves

METHOD

Combine the apple juice and grape juice in a large saucepan. Bring to a boil, turn down the heat, and simmer until the juice has reduced by one-half. Add the remaining ingredients, return to a boil, and then simmer gently for 1 hour, stirring frequently or until the chutney has thickened.

Remove the chili pepper before ladling into jars.

Tomato-Onion Chutney

The complex flavor combinations in this excellent recipe are unusual enough to satisfy chutney experts but will also please less adventurous appetites.

YIELD: **6 pints**
PACK: **Hot**
HEADSPACE: **¼ inch**
PROCESSING TIME: **20 minutes**

INGREDIENTS

- 14 tomatoes, peeled, cored, and chopped
- 2 cups peeled, chopped onion
- 6 tart green apples, peeled, cored, and chopped
- 2 cucumbers, peeled and chopped
- 2 red bell peppers, seeded and chopped
- 1¼ cups raisins
- 2¾ cups packed brown sugar
- 1 small red chili pepper, seeded and chopped
- 2 garlic cloves, peeled and minced
- 1 teaspoon salt
- 3 cups distilled white vinegar
- 1 tablespoon peeled, minced gingerroot
- 2 cinnamon sticks, broken into pieces
- 4 allspice berries

METHOD

In a large saucepan, combine all the ingredients except for the cinnamon-stick pieces and allspice berries. Tie these spices in a muslin or cheesecloth bag and add the bag to the mixture. Bring to a boil and simmer slowly, stirring frequently, for 1½ hours or until the chutney has thickened. Remove the spice bag before ladling into jars.

Green Mango and Apple Chutney

We're especially fond of this recipe not only because it's so tasty, but also because it calls for green mangoes, which in our area of the country are much easier to find than ripe ones!

YIELD: **8 half-pints**
PACK: **Hot**
HEADSPACE: **½ inch**
PROCESSING TIME: **20 minutes**

INGREDIENTS

- 10 green mangoes
- 2 garlic cloves, peeled and minced
- 1 hot chili pepper, seeded and chopped
- ½ cup raisins
- ½ cup currants
- 2¼ cups cider vinegar
- 2 tart green apples
- 2 tablespoons salt
- 2½ cups packed brown sugar
- 2 tablespoons lemon juice
- 2 tablespoons grated lemon peel
- 2 tablespoons peeled, minced gingerroot

METHOD

Peel the mangoes, slice the flesh from the pits, and chop. In a large bowl, combine the mangoes, garlic, chili pepper, raisins, and currants with 1 cup of the vinegar. Cover the bowl and allow it to stand at room temperature for 24 hours.

Peel, core, and chop the apples. In a large saucepan, combine the apples with the mango mixture, salt, brown sugar, lemon juice and peel, ginger, and remaining vinegar. Bring to a boil, turn down the heat, and simmer, stirring frequently, for up to 4 hours or until the chutney has thickened. Ladle into jars.

Ripe Mango and Apple Chutney

The best-known of tropical fruit flavors must surely be that of ripe mangoes. To ripen green mangoes for this gloriously rich and chunky chutney, place them in a paper bag and let them stand at room temperature for two or three days.

YIELD: **6 pints**
PACK: **Hot**
HEADSPACE: **¼ inch**
PROCESSING TIME: **10 minutes**

INGREDIENTS

- 8 ripe mangoes
- 8 whole cloves
- 8 allspice berries
- 8 cardamom seeds
- 2 cinnamon sticks, broken into pieces
- 2 tart green apples, peeled, cored, and chopped
- 2 onions, peeled and chopped
- 3 garlic cloves, peeled and minced
- 2½ cups packed brown sugar
- 1 cup golden raisins
- 1 tablespoon peeled, minced gingerroot
- 1¾ cups cider vinegar
- ½ cup lime juice
- 2 small red chili peppers, seeded

METHOD

Peel the mangoes, slice the flesh from the pits, and chop into large chunks. Set aside the cloves, allspice, cardamom, and cinnamon-stick pieces. Then combine the mangoes with the remaining ingredients and allow them to stand overnight.

Place the mango mixture in a large saucepan. Tie the reserved spices in a cheesecloth or muslin bag and suspend them in the mixture. Bring the mixture to a boil, turn down the heat, and simmer, stirring frequently, for about 30 minutes; the chutney should thicken considerably. Remove the two chili peppers and the spice bag before ladling the hot chutney into jars.

Rhubarb-Kumquat Chutney

Creative combinations of ingredients can result in astoundingly delicious chutneys. The two tart fruits in this chutney blend perfectly.

YIELD: **5 pints**
PACK: **Hot**
HEADSPACE: **¼ inch**
PROCESSING TIME: **20 minutes**

INGREDIENTS

1¼ pounds kumquats
1½ cups granulated sugar
1 cup water
1 cinnamon stick, broken into pieces
6 allspice berries
1¾ pounds rhubarb, chopped
3 onions, peeled and chopped
2 hot or sweet peppers, peeled, seeded, and chopped
3 garlic cloves, peeled and minced
1½ cups raisins
6 cups packed brown sugar
6 cups distilled white vinegar
Grated peel and juice of 2 lemons
1 tablespoon peeled, minced gingerroot
2 teaspoons curry powder
1 tablespoon salt

METHOD

Rinse the kumquats in hot water. To prepare them, slice them in half along their lengths and remove their seeds. Then combine them with the granulated sugar and water in a large saucepan. Bring to a boil, turn down the heat, and simmer for 45 minutes.

Tie the cinnamon-stick pieces and allspice berries in a muslin or cheesecloth bag. Add the bag and all the remaining ingredients to the simmering kumquats. Continue to simmer until thick (for about 2 hours), stirring frequently. Remove the spice bag before ladling into jars.

Nectarine-Peach Chutney

Simple, sweet, and made with fruit juice instead of sugar, this chutney works miracles with meatless curries.

YIELD: **6 pints**
PACK: **Hot**
HEADSPACE: **½ inch**
PROCESSING TIME: **10 minutes**

INGREDIENTS

1½ pounds nectarines, peeled, pitted, and finely sliced
1½ pounds peaches, peeled, pitted, and finely sliced
1 pound red onions, peeled and chopped
6 tablespoons peeled, minced gingerroot
3½ cups orange juice
¼ cup lemon juice
2 tablespoons grated orange peel
1 tablespoon grated lemon peel
1 cup distilled white vinegar
4 cups golden raisins
1 teaspoon cinnamon
½ teaspoon cayenne pepper
2 teaspoons salt

METHOD

Combine all the ingredients in a large saucepan. Bring to a boil, reduce the heat, and simmer, stirring frequently, for about 45 minutes or until the chutney has thickened. Ladle into jars.

Catherine's Fruit Chutney

If you've never tasted a chutney before, this excellent recipe is a great place to start. The classic combination of fruits will acquaint your taste buds with a typically tasty chutney blend.

YIELD: **7 half-pints**
PACK: **Hot**
HEADSPACE: **½ inch**
PROCESSING TIME: **10 minutes**

INGREDIENTS

1 lemon
2 cups cider vinegar
1 pound brown sugar
2 garlic cloves, peeled and minced
⅛ teaspoon mixed cayenne pepper and chili powder
1½ teaspoons salt
5½ cups peeled, cored, and chopped apples, pears, and peaches
¾ cup minced, crystallized ginger
1½ cups raisins

METHOD

Mince the lemon, both pulp and peel, discarding the seeds but retaining the juice. Combine the minced lemon and its juice with the vinegar, brown sugar, garlic, cayenne pepper, chili powder, and salt. Bring to a boil, lower the heat, and simmer for 30 minutes, stirring frequently.

Add the fresh fruit, ginger, and raisins, and simmer for another 30 to 45 minutes, stirring frequently to prevent scorching. The fruit should be soft, but not mushy, when you ladle the chutney into jars.

Citrus and Mustard Chutney

The distinctive flavor of this chutney complements cheese dishes and cold meats better than curries.

YIELD: **7 half-pints**

PACK: **Hot**

HEADSPACE: **½ inch**

PROCESSING TIME: **10 minutes**

INGREDIENTS

  5 whole lemons, seeded and finely sliced

  3 whole oranges, seeded and finely sliced

  1 whole lime, seeded and finely sliced

  1 pound onions, peeled and finely sliced

  6 tablespoons salt

  1 tart green apple, peeled, cored, and chopped

1⅓ cups golden raisins

  4 cups sugar

  3 cups distilled white vinegar

  ¼ cup mustard seed

  2 tablespoons peeled, minced gingerroot

  ½ teaspoon cayenne pepper

METHOD

In a large mixing bowl, arrange the lemon, orange, lime, and onion slices in layers, sprinkling some of the salt over each layer. Place a large plate on top of the slices and position two or three water-filled jars on top of the plate to press the layers together. Cover the bowl with plastic wrap and let stand at room temperature for 24 hours. Removing the excess moisture in this fashion is a necessary first step, so don't be tempted to skip it!

To remove the excess salt, transfer the slices to a plastic colander, rinse well under cold running water, and drain. Then place the drained slices in a large saucepan and barely cover with water. Bring to a boil, lower the heat, and simmer gently, stirring occasionally, for about 30 minutes or until the citrus peels are soft.

Add the remaining ingredients, return to a boil, lower the heat, and simmer gently for another 40 to 45 minutes. Be sure to stir the chutney frequently in order to prevent scorching as it reduces and thickens. Ladle into jars.

Spiced Pear Chutney

Especially rich chutneys should be shamelessly served with equally rich foods. Try this one with roast pork.

YIELD: **7 half-pints**

PACK: **Hot**

HEADSPACE: **¼ inch**

PROCESSING TIME: **10 minutes**

INGREDIENTS

  1 cinnamon stick, broken into pieces

  6 allspice berries

12 whole cloves

10 pears, peeled, cored, and chopped

  ½ cup golden raisins

  ½ cup peeled, chopped red onion

1½ cups packed brown sugar

  2 tablespoons mustard seed

  2 tablespoons peeled, minced gingerroot

  1 teaspoon salt

  2 garlic cloves, peeled and minced

  1 small red chili pepper, seeded and chopped

  2 cups cider vinegar

METHOD

Tie the cinnamon-stick pieces, allspice berries, and cloves in a muslin or cheesecloth bag. In a large saucepan, combine all the remaining ingredients and add the spice bag to them. Bring the mixture to a boil. Reduce the heat and simmer, stirring frequently, for 45 minutes or until the chutney has thickened. Remove the spice bag before ladling into jars.

Almond-Prune Chutney

A most unusual but tasty chutney, this is an excellent addition to ham dishes and even works well as a glaze.

YIELD: **7 half-pints**

PACK: **Hot**

HEADSPACE: **¼ inch**

PROCESSING TIME: **10 minutes**

INGREDIENTS

2 pounds prunes

2 pounds tart green apples, peeled, cored, and chopped

¼ cup water

2 cups packed brown sugar

2 cinnamon sticks, broken into pieces

4 allspice berries

1 green chili pepper, seeded

2 cups blanched, slivered almonds

2½ cups cider vinegar

2 teaspoons curry powder

METHOD

To soften the prunes, cover them with boiling water and allow them to stand overnight. Drain well, remove the pits, and chop.

Place the apples in a large saucepan and add the water and ½ cup of the brown sugar. Tie the cinnamon-stick pieces and allspice berries in a muslin or cheesecloth bag and add the bag to the mixture, along with the green chili pepper. Bring to a simmer, stirring to dissolve the sugar, and then simmer until the apples are soft.

Add the chopped prunes, slivered almonds, vinegar, and curry powder. Bring the mixture to a boil, reduce the heat, and simmer for about 40 minutes or until the chutney has thickened. (Don't forget to stir, or the chutney will scorch.) Remove the spice bag and chili pepper before ladling into jars.

Traditional Indian Chutney

Often called Bengal chutney, this popular north Indian recipe, which dates back to the days of the British Empire, can be found, in one form or another, in many cookbooks.

YIELD: **6 half-pints**

PACK: **Hot**

HEADSPACE: **½ inch**

PROCESSING TIME: **10 minutes**

INGREDIENTS

6 carrots, peeled and chopped

2 onions, peeled and chopped

4 tart green apples, peeled, cored, and chopped

1⅓ cups raisins

½ pound peeled, grated horseradish

2 cups packed brown sugar

2 tablespoons salt

2 tablespoons peeled, minced gingerroot

2 tablespoons curry powder

1 teaspoon dry mustard

1 teaspoon mace

2½ cups distilled white vinegar

Combine all the ingredients in a large saucepan. Bring to a boil, turn down the heat, and simmer, stirring frequently, for about 1 hour or until the chutney thickens. Ladle into jars.

Dawn's Pineapple Chutney

Many chutneys require freshly harvested produce. This one, however, can be made with ingredients available even in the dead of winter.

YIELD: **6 pints**

PACK: **Hot**

HEADSPACE: **¼ inch**

PROCESSING TIME: **20 minutes**

INGREDIENTS

53 ounces canned, crushed pineapple in juice

2½ cups cider vinegar

1 cup water

1 cup chopped, pickled jalapeño peppers

¼ cup soy sauce

½ cup dried onion flakes

3 scallions, sliced

½ red bell pepper, seeded and chopped

1¼ cups packed brown sugar

½ pound raisins

1 tablespoon ginger

1 tablespoon curry powder

1 tablespoon mustard seed

1½ teaspoons coarsely ground black pepper

1½ teaspoons red pepper flakes

METHOD

Combine all the ingredients in a large saucepan and bring to a boil. Reduce the heat and simmer, stirring frequently, for about 30 to 45 minutes or until the chutney has thickened. Ladle into jars.

Jennifer's Winter Chutney

Here's another great chutney recipe that's tailored to bring some joy to a cold winter day. All its ingredients are available from the grocery store year-round.

YIELD: **6 half-pints**
PACK: **Hot**
HEADSPACE: **¼ inch**
PROCESSING TIME: **10 minutes**

INGREDIENTS

- 1½ pounds pears, peeled, cored, and chopped
- 1½ pounds apples, peeled, cored, and chopped
- 1 cup distilled white vinegar
- 1 cup granulated sugar
- ½ cup packed brown sugar
- 2½ tablespoons peeled, minced gingerroot
- 3 tablespoons lemon juice
- 1 tablespoon grated lemon peel
- 1 teaspoon salt
- ¾ teaspoon cayenne pepper
- ¼ teaspoon cinnamon
- 1½ cups fresh cranberries

METHOD

In a large saucepan, combine all the ingredients except for the cranberries. Bring to a boil over high heat. Reduce the heat to low and simmer, stirring occasionally, for about 25 minutes or until the fruit is almost translucent.

Add the cranberries and continue to simmer until the skins of the cranberries pop open. Skim and discard any foam from the top before ladling into jars.

Georgia's Carolina Chow-Chow

Georgia's crisp cabbage chow-chow includes no hot peppers but is rich with flavorful spices.

INGREDIENTS

- 1 gallon chopped cabbage
- 2 quarts cored, chopped green tomatoes
- 12 red bell peppers, seeded and chopped
- 12 sweet green peppers, seeded and chopped
- 12 onions, peeled and chopped
- ½ cup salt
- 2 tablespoons mixed pickling spices
- 2 quarts distilled white vinegar
- 5 cups sugar
- 2 tablespoons mustard
- 1 teaspoon turmeric
- 1 tablespoon ginger
- 2 tablespoons mustard seed
- 5 tablespoons celery seed

YIELD: **7 quarts**
PACK: **Hot**
HEADSPACE: **½ inch**
PROCESSING TIME: **10 minutes**

METHOD

Combine the cabbage, tomatoes, peppers, onions, and salt in a large bowl, mixing the salt in well, and let stand for 4 hours.

Tie the mixed pickling spices in a muslin or cheesecloth bag. Place the bag in a large saucepan, along with the vinegar, sugar, and remaining spices. Bring the mixture to a boil, lower the heat, and simmer for 10 minutes. Drain the tomatoes, pepper, and onions well, add them to the simmering mixture, and cook until the tomatoes and vegetables have been thoroughly heated. Remove the spice bag and ladle the chow-chowd into jars.

Bengal Chow-Chow

A very old recipe, this curry-flavored relish makes a fine condiment for both cold and hot meat dishes.

YIELD: **4 pints**
PACK: **Hot**
HEADSPACE: **¼ inch**
PROCESSING TIME: **10 minutes**

INGREDIENTS

 1 head cauliflower
 3 sweet green peppers, seeded and chopped
 1 small red chili pepper, seeded and chopped
 3 cucumbers, peeled and chopped
 ½ cup salt
 1 quart water
 1 cup sugar
 3 tablespoons flour
 2 tablespoons mustard seed
 2 tablespoons curry powder
 1 teaspoon turmeric
 1 quart distilled white vinegar

METHOD

Remove the core from the cauliflower and separate the florets, chopping large ones into smaller pieces. Then place all the vegetables in a large bowl, sprinkle with the salt, and cover with 1 quart of water. Cover the bowl and leave it in the refrigerator for 8 to 10 hours.

Combine the remaining ingredients in a large saucepan, adding the vinegar gradually while stirring the dry ingredients so that the flour won't turn into lumps. Bring to a boil, then simmer, stirring, until the mixture thickens. Drain the brined vegetables well and add them to the simmering mixture. Continue to simmer for 10 minutes before ladling into jars.

Susie's Kentucky Piccalilli

We're not sure how piccalilli got it's name, but this traditional relish, which is made with green tomatoes, is a real treat. Susie heats or fries hers before serving it.

YIELD: **6 pints**
PACK: **Hot**
HEADSPACE: **½ inch**
PROCESSING TIME: **10 minutes**

INGREDIENTS

 1 quart cored, chopped green tomatoes
 1 quart chopped cabbage
 2 sweet green peppers, seeded and chopped
 2 red bell peppers, seeded and chopped
 2 onions, peeled and chopped
 ¼ cup salt
 2 cups packed brown sugar
 ½ cup salt
 1½ cups water
 1 teaspoon dried mustard
 1 teaspoon turmeric
 1 teaspoon celery seed
 1½ cups distilled white vinegar

METHOD

Place the tomatoes, cabbage, peppers, and onions in a large bowl. Mix them with the salt and allow them to stand overnight. Drain well, then press in a clean cloth or towel to remove all excess moisture.

In a large saucepan, combine the remaining ingredients, bring them to a boil, and boil for 5 minutes. Add the tomatoes and vegetables, and return to a boil before ladling into jars.

Spiced Piccalilli

The spices in this relish make it a bit unusual but very tasty nonetheless. For an even spicier version, add a seeded, chopped chili pepper.

YIELD: **8 pints**
PACK: **Hot**
HEADSPACE: **¼ inch**
PROCESSING TIME: **15 minutes**

INGREDIENTS

 20 tomatoes, peeled, cored, and chopped
 8 sweet green peppers, seeded and chopped
 4 red bell peppers, seeded and chopped
 2 onions, peeled and chopped
 6 cups cider vinegar
 4 whole cloves
 5 allspice berries
 1 cinnamon stick, broken into pieces
 3½ cups sugar
 ⅓ cup salt
 1 tablespoon celery seed
 ⅓ cup mustard seed

METHOD

Combine the tomatoes, peppers, onions, and 2 cups of the vinegar in a large saucepan. Tie the cloves, allspice berries, and cinnamon-stick pieces in a muslin or cheese-cloth bag and add it to the saucepan as well. Bring to a boil and boil for 30 minutes, stirring frequently.

Drain the vegetables well, return them to the saucepan, and add the remaining vinegar and ingredients. Also include the spice bag. Bring to a boil and simmer for 5 minutes. Remove the spice bag before ladling the piccalilli into jars.

salsas and savory sauces

SPICY OR MILD, chunky or creamy, green, red, or golden brown, the foods in this chapter are ones we classify as "comfort" foods—the kinds that transform gloomy days into days worth living. When you're down in the dumps, dunking a warm tortilla chip into a bowl of zesty salsa or feasting on warm pasta with homemade marinara sauce are incomparably nurturing activities, especially when the chopping, slicing, dicing, skimming, and simmering have already been done.

You'll notice that some of these recipes can be processed in a boiling-water bath, while others must be pressure canned. Just refer to previous chapters for instructions on processing methods. Every recipe includes the

- recipe yield by number and size of jars
- recommended style of pack
- required headspace
- required processing time
- required pressure, if the recipe must be pressure canned.

If you live more than 1,000 feet above sea level, don't forget to make the required processing time and/or pressure adjustments (see pages 45 and 53).

Coward's Green Salsa

For those of you who fall into the perfectly acceptable class of hot-pepper sissies, here's a very mild but flavorful green salsa.

YIELD: **5 pints**

PACK: **Hot**

HEADSPACE: **½ inch**

PROCESSING TIME: **15 minutes**

INGREDIENTS

3 cups husked, chopped tomatillos

2 cups chopped green tomatoes

½ cup seeded, chopped long green chili peppers

1½ cups seeded, chopped sweet green peppers

4 cups chopped onions

½ cup lemon juice

½ cup lime juice

6 cloves garlic, peeled and minced

1 tablespoon cumin

2 tablespoons oregano

2 teaspoons salt

4 crushed black peppercorns

METHOD

Combine all the ingredients in a saucepan and bring to a boil. Reduce the heat and simmer for about 20 minutes before ladling into jars.

Recipe Tips

■ Once they're heat processed, the chopped ingredients in pressure-canned foods tend to be soft in texture. If you prefer chunkier textures, add fresh vegetables to the opened jars of salsa or sauce before serving them.

■ Paste tomatoes, such as Roma, stay firmer and less watery in home-canned tomato products. We recommend them highly for salsas.

■ Many salsa recipes call for fresh cilantro. For truly fresh flavors, add a bit more of this herb as a garnish just before serving.

■ Peeling tomatoes is easy. First dunk them in boiling water for 30 to 40 seconds. Then quickly submerge them in cold water, drain them well, and peel away the loosened skins.

Beginner's Salsa

This recipe, a fine one for salsa neophytes, includes the typical— and typically delicious—combination of tomatoes, peppers, and onions.

YIELD: **6 half-pints**

PACK: **Hot**

HEADSPACE: **½ inch**

PROCESSING TIME: **30 minutes**

INGREDIENTS

4 cups peeled, cored, and chopped tomatoes

2½ cups seeded, chopped sweet green peppers

¾ cup seeded, chopped chili peppers

½ cup peeled, chopped onion

1 teaspoon salt

3 cloves garlic, peeled and minced

1¾ cups distilled white vinegar

1 teaspoon black pepper

METHOD

In a saucepan, combine all the ingredients and bring to a boil. Turn down the heat and simmer, stirring frequently, for 20 minutes or until thick. Ladle into jars.

Catherine's Salsa

The jalapeños in this salsa are fiery indeed, so you may want to label gift jars with a friendly warning!

YIELD: **7 pints**

PACK: **Hot**

HEADSPACE: **½ inch**

PROCESSING TIME: **25 minutes**

INGREDIENTS

5 pounds tomatoes, peeled, cored, seeded, and chopped

1½ pounds onions, peeled and chopped

12 cloves garlic, peeled and minced

1–2 pounds jalapeño peppers, seeded and chopped

¾ cup cider vinegar

¾ cup lemon juice

2 teaspoons salt

1 cup chopped, loosely packed fresh cilantro

METHOD

In a large saucepan, combine all the ingredients except the cilantro. Bring to a boil and simmer for 10 minutes. Stir in the cilantro and return to a boil before ladling into jars.

Devil's Delight Salsa

A first taste of this salsa may bring as many curses to your lips as it brings tears to your eyes. It certainly brings new meaning to the word "hot," so don't say we didn't warn you!

YIELD: **7 pints**
PACK: **Hot**
HEADSPACE: **½ inch**
PROCESSING TIME: **15 minutes**

INGREDIENTS

- 3 quarts peeled, cored, and chopped tomatoes
- 3 cups peeled, chopped onions
- 6 small hot peppers, seeded and minced
- 4 long green chili peppers, seeded and chopped
- 4 cloves garlic, peeled and minced
- 2 12-ounce cans tomato paste
- 2 cups lemon juice
- 2 teaspoons salt
- 2 teaspoons brown sugar
- 1½ tablespoons cumin
- 6 crushed black peppercorns

METHOD

Combine all the ingredients in a large saucepan and bring to a boil. Reduce the heat and simmer, stirring occasionally, for 30 minutes or until thick. Ladle into jars.

Count-The-Peppers Salsa

The trick to this fine salsa is combining five different types of peppers: sweet green or yellow, red bell, and three varieties of hot peppers. We leave the choice of hot peppers to you, but suggest that you choose at least one mild variety or you may find the salsa too fiery to be flavorful.

YIELD: **6 to 8 pints**
PACK: **Hot**
HEADSPACE: **½ inch**
PROCESSING TIME: **15 minutes**

INGREDIENTS

- 10 cups peeled, cored, and chopped tomatoes
- 2 cups seeded, chopped sweet green and red bell peppers
- 4 cups seeded, chopped hot peppers
- ¾ cup vinegar
- ¼ cup lime juice
- 2 teaspoons salt
- 6 crushed black peppercorns

METHOD

Combine all the ingredients in a saucepan and bring to a boil. Lower the heat and simmer for 10 minutes before ladling into jars.

Jalapeño Chili Sauce

A truly hot sauce for lovers of fiery foods, this one can be processed in a boiling-water bath because it's basically a pickled product.

YIELD: **7 pints**
PACK: **Hot**
HEADSPACE: **½ inch**
PROCESSING TIME: **15 minutes**

INGREDIENTS

28	tomatoes, peeled, cored, and chopped
2¼	cups peeled, chopped onions
2¼	cups seeded, chopped red bell peppers
1	jalapeño pepper, seeded and chopped
1¼	cups sugar
2½	tablespoons salt
3	tablespoons mixed pickling spices
1	tablespoon celery seed
2¾	cups distilled white vinegar

METHOD

In a stockpot, combine the tomatoes, onions, peppers, sugar, and salt. Bring to a boil, lower the heat, and simmer gently for about 50 minutes. Place the pickling spices and celery seed in a spice bag and suspend the bag in the tomato mixture. Continue to cook, stirring frequently to prevent sticking, until the volume of the sauce has reduced by half.

Add the vinegar and continue to simmer gently, stirring frequently, until the sauce has thickened as desired. Remove the spice bag before ladling into jars.

Black Bean and Corn Sauce

On the basis of its taste, this recipe could be classified as a Mexican salsa, but it's a bit too liquid to serve in dollops. You'll find that it's best ladled generously over enchiladas or steamed rice.

YIELD: **7 pints**
PACK: **Hot**
HEADSPACE: **1 inch**
DIAL-GAUGE CANNER
  TIME & PRESSURE: **85 minutes/11 pounds**
WEIGHTED-GAUGE CANNER
  TIME & PRESSURE: **85 minutes/10 pounds**

INGREDIENTS

5¼	cups dried black beans
4	garlic cloves, peeled and minced
1	cup peeled, chopped onions
2	teaspoons salt
7	cups corn kernels, fresh or frozen
2	cups seeded, chopped sweet green peppers
2	jalapeño peppers, seeded and chopped
½	cup water
½	cup balsamic vinegar
¼	cup lime juice
¼	cup olive oil
2	teaspoons sugar
1	teaspoon dried coriander
¾	cup chopped, loosely packed fresh cilantro

METHOD

Cover the beans in water and soak them overnight. Drain and place the beans in a saucepan. Add the garlic, onion, and salt, cover with fresh water, and bring to boil. Lower the heat and cook for about 1 hour. The beans should be tender but not soft. Drain well.

In a large saucepan, combine the beans with the corn, peppers, and ½ cup of water. Bring to a boil, turn down the heat, and simmer gently for 10 minutes. Then add the remaining ingredients, return to a boil, and cook for another 20 minutes or until thick before ladling into jars.

Roasted Chili Sauce

Serve this delicious hot sauce in small portions with grilled meats, chicken, or fish.

YIELD: **7 half-pints**

PACK: **Hot**

HEADSPACE: **½ inch**

DIAL-GAUGE CANNER
  TIME & PRESSURE: **35 minutes/11 pounds**

WEIGHTED-GAUGE CANNER
  TIME & PRESSURE: **35 minutes/10 pounds**

INGREDIENTS

  7 long green chili peppers

  3 onions, peeled and chopped

10 garlic cloves, peeled and minced

  6 tablespoons olive oil

  6 tomatoes, peeled, cored, and chopped

  ½ cup tomato paste

  ¼ cup lemon juice

  1 tablespoon grated lemon peel

  2 teaspoons salt

  2 teaspoons dried coriander

  1 teaspoon chili powder

METHOD

To roast the chili peppers, place them on a baking sheet and broil them about 5 inches away from the heat for 30 minutes, turning them every few minutes to brown them evenly. Remove the peppers from the oven and allow them to cool. Then slip off the skins and remove the stems and seeds. Using a food processor or blender, puree the roasted peppers.

Sauté the onions and garlic in the olive oil until tender. Then combine them, in a saucepan, with the pureed peppers and remaining ingredients and bring to a boil. Reduce the heat and simmer for 15 minutes or until thick before ladling into jars.

Sweet and Spicy Seafood Sauce

Superb with fish, this fruit-based sauce is also excellent with cold meats and in salad dressings. Add a few minced cilantro or mint leaves just before serving it.

YIELD: **7 pints**

PACK: **Hot**

HEADSPACE: **1 inch**

DIAL-GAUGE CANNER
  TIME & PRESSURE: **40 minutes/11 pounds**

WEIGHTED-GAUGE CANNER
  TIME & PRESSURE: **40 minutes/10 pounds**

INGREDIENTS

  7 ripe mangoes, peeled, pitted, and chopped

  7 papayas, peeled, seeded, and chopped

  7 jalapeño peppers, seeded and chopped

  5 tablespoons peeled, minced gingerroot

  2 oranges, peeled, membranes removed, seeded, and chopped

3½ cups unsweetened pineapple juice

  ½ cup lime juice

  ¼ cup distilled white vinegar

  2 teaspoons salt

METHOD

Combine all the ingredients in a large saucepan and bring to a boil. Turn down the heat and simmer for 20 minutes or until thick before ladling into jars.

Hot Peppers

Hot-pepper devotees know that each of the many varieties has its own characteristics. Following are thumbnail descriptions of a few common peppers, but feel free to make substitutions in our recipes.

■ *Anaheim: Mild; medium long; green to orange; very flavorful*

■ *Cayenne: Very hot; short to medium long; bright red; more heat than flavor*

■ *Habañero: Extremely hot; short; green to orange; flavorful*

■ *Hungarian wax: Mild to hot; short; yellow; quite flavorful*

■ *Jalapeño: Very hot; short; green to red; flavorful*

■ *Serrano: Very hot; short; green; flavorful*

When a recipe calls for long green chili peppers, choose a mild variety. Ancho and Colorado, as well as Anaheim and Hungarian wax, are good choices.

Kalamata Olive Sauce

Serve this salsa-like, olive-laced sauce hot on Italian pastas or cold on crisp green salads.

YIELD: **7 half-pints**
PACK: **Hot**
HEADSPACE: **½ inch**
DIAL-GAUGE CANNER
  TIME & PRESSURE: **35 minutes/11 pounds**
WEIGHTED-GAUGE CANNER
  TIME & PRESSURE: **35 minutes/10 pounds**

INGREDIENTS

¾ pound pitted, chopped
  Kalamata olives

¾ pound pitted, chopped large
  green olives

1½ cups seeded, chopped sweet
  green peppers

1 cup sun-dried tomatoes,
  broken into pieces

2 teaspoons dried oregano

2 tablespoons chopped
  fresh basil

3 garlic cloves, peeled and
  minced

2 tablespoons balsamic
  vinegar

2 tablespoons distilled white
  vinegar

¾ cup olive oil

6 crushed black peppercorns

METHOD

Combine all the ingredients in a large saucepan and bring to a boil. Turn down the heat and simmer for 30 minutes or until thick before ladling into jars.

Red Sauce

A wonderful country recipe, this garden-fresh sweet-and-sour sauce is the perfect complement to family pot-roast dinners.

YIELD: **7 pints**
PACK: **Hot**
HEADSPACE: **1 inch**
PROCESSING TIME: **15 minutes**

INGREDIENTS

8 pounds tomatoes, peeled,
  cored, and chopped

1 tablespoon salt

6 red bell peppers

½ head red cabbage

4 red apples

3 cups sugar

2 cups distilled white vinegar

1 tablespoon salt

2 tablespoons mixed pickling
  spices

METHOD

Mix the tomatoes and 1 tablespoon of salt in a large bowl. Cover and let stand for 4 hours. Rinse, drain well, and place in a large stockpot.

Seed and chop the peppers; core and chop the cabbage; and peel, core, and chop the apples. Add these ingredients to the tomatoes, along with the sugar, vinegar, and salt. Tie the pickling spices in a muslin or cheesecloth bag and add the bag as well. Bring to a boil, lower the heat, and simmer, stirring frequently, for 45 minutes or until thick. Remove the spice bag before ladling into jars.

Green Chili Taco Sauce

Dedicated to folks who like it hot, this taco sauce is great on tacos, burritos, tortilla chips, and more.

YIELD: **7 pints**
PACK: **Hot**
HEADSPACE: **1 inch**
DIAL-GAUGE CANNER
  TIME & PRESSURE: **20 minutes/11 pounds**
WEIGHTED-GAUGE CANNER
  TIME & PRESSURE: **20 minutes/10 pounds**

INGREDIENTS

2 pounds long green chili
  peppers

9 pounds tomatoes, peeled
  and chopped

1½ cups peeled, chopped onions

3 garlic cloves, peeled and
  minced

1 teaspoon salt

1 teaspoon sugar

2 teaspoons oregano

1 tablespoon lime juice

METHOD

Slit the peppers lengthwise and broil for about 6 minutes or until the skins blister. After the peppers have cooled, peel them, remove the seeds, and chop.

Combine all the ingredients in a large stockpot and bring to a boil. Simmer for 15 minutes, stirring frequently, then ladle into jars.

YIELD: **7 half-pints**

PACK: **Hot**

HEADSPACE: ¹⁄₂ **inch**

DIAL-GAUGE CANNER
   TIME & PRESSURE: **35 minutes/11 pounds**

WEIGHTED-GAUGE CANNER
   TIME & PRESSURE: **35 minutes/10 pounds**

Haitian Hot Sauce

This spicy vegetable sauce has more than a touch of lime in it and tastes especially good on fish, chicken, or pork.

INGREDIENTS

7 onions, peeled and chopped

7 shallots, peeled and chopped

2 red bell peppers, seeded and chopped

3 tomatoes, peeled, cored, and chopped

1 cup lime juice

1 cup distilled white vinegar

¹⁄₂ cup olive oil

¹⁄₂ teaspoon cayenne pepper

¹⁄₂ tablespoon salt

¹⁄₂ teaspoon pepper

METHOD

Combine all the ingredients and refrigerate for 48 hours so that the flavors will blend together. Place in a large saucepan, bring to a boil, then simmer for 5 minutes before ladling into jars.

Spicy Tomato Catsup

The word "catsup," believe it or not, is derived from the Chinese word meaning "brine of pickled fish." We'll spare you the original recipe. Today's catsups are smooth, pourable sauces, usually, but not always, made with tomatoes.

YIELD: **7 pints**

PACK: **Hot**

HEADSPACE: ¹⁄₄ **inch**

PROCESSING TIME: **10 minutes**

INGREDIENTS

9 quarts cored, chopped tomatoes

1¹⁄₂ cups peeled, chopped onions

2 cups seeded, chopped red bell peppers

1 small red chili pepper, seeded and chopped

2 garlic cloves, peeled and minced

3 cups cider vinegar

8 allspice berries

1 cinnamon stick, broken into pieces

6 crushed black peppercorns

2 tablespoons celery seed

2 teaspoons mustard seed

1¹⁄₂ cups brown sugar

2 tablespoons paprika

Salt to taste

METHOD

In a stockpot, combine the tomatoes, onions, peppers, and garlic. Bring to a boil and cook over high heat, uncovered, for about 20 minutes or until the vegetables are soft. Press through a sieve or strainer and return to the stockpot.

Pour the vinegar into a small saucepan. Tie the five whole spices in a muslin or cheesecloth bag and add the bag to the vinegar. Bring to a boil and simmer for 10 minutes. Remove the spice bag and add the vinegar to the vegetable mixture, along with the brown sugar, paprika, and salt. Bring to a boil, lower the heat, and simmer for about 30 minutes or until the catsup has reduced by half and is fairly thick. Ladle into jars.

Basil Marinara Sauce

This sauce goes best with fresh pasta, of course, but it's so rich with basil and red wine that it turns even ordinary spaghetti into a gourmet feast.

YIELD: **7 pints**

PACK: **Hot**

HEADSPACE: **1 inch**

DIAL-GAUGE CANNER
TIME & PRESSURE: **25 minutes/11 pounds**

WEIGHTED-GAUGE CANNER
TIME & PRESSURE: **25 minutes/10 pounds**

INGREDIENTS

20 pounds tomatoes, peeled, cored, and chopped

3¼ cups peeled, chopped onions

1 cup grated carrot

9 garlic cloves, peeled and minced

½ cup chopped fresh basil leaves

2 tablespoons oregano

1 tablespoon sugar

2 teaspoons salt

½ teaspoon black pepper

2¼ cups red wine

3 tablespoons lemon juice

6 tablespoons olive oil

METHOD

In a large stockpot, combine the tomatoes, onions, carrot, garlic, basil, and oregano. Bring to a boil, turn down the heat, and cover. Simmer gently, stirring occasionally, for 1 hour or until the sauce begins to thicken. Allow the sauce to cool, then run through a food mill or sieve to remove seeds and skins.

Return the puree to the stockpot and add the remaining ingredients. Simmer gently, uncovered, for about 2 hours or until the volume has reduced by half. To prevent scorching, be sure to stir frequently. Ladle into jars.

Horseradish and Green Tomato Sauce

Recipes for good horseradish sauces aren't easy to find. We came by this one in a very old cookbook and adapted it to conform to contemporary tastes.

YIELD: **7 half-pints**

PACK: **Hot**

HEADSPACE: **½ inch**

PROCESSING TIME: **20 minutes**

INGREDIENTS

1½ pounds green tomatoes, cored

1 pound onions, peeled

½ pound sweet green peppers, seeded

3 tablespoons salt

2¾ cups cider vinegar

1 cinnamon stick, broken into pieces

4 whole allspice berries

4 whole cloves

1 cup packed brown sugar

1¼ cups peeled, grated horseradish

METHOD

In a blender or food processor, coarsely grind the tomatoes, onions, and peppers. In a large bowl, combine these ingredients with the salt and allow them to stand overnight. Rinse well and drain.

Pour the vinegar into a small saucepan. Tie the whole spices in a muslin or cheesecloth bag and add the bag to the vinegar. Bring to a boil and simmer for 15 minutes to infuse the vinegar with the spice flavors. Discard the spice bag when done.

In a large saucepan, combine the drained vegetables with the vinegar and brown sugar. Bring to a boil, lower the heat, and simmer for about 50 minutes or until the sauce has thickened. Then add the horseradish and continue to simmer for another 5 or 10 minutes. Ladle into jars when thick.

Tuscan Pasta Sauce

*Or, in the language of long ago, spaghetti sauce—
and one of the finest we've ever tasted.*

YIELD: **7 pints**

PACK: **Hot**

HEADSPACE: **1 inch**

DIAL-GAUGE CANNER
 TIME & PRESSURE: **20 minutes/11 pounds**

WEIGHTED-GAUGE CANNER
 TIME & PRESSURE: **20 minutes/10 pounds**

INGREDIENTS

- 25 pounds tomatoes, cored and chopped
- 3 tablespoons olive oil
- 1 cup chopped celery
- ¾ cup peeled, chopped onion
- 5 garlic cloves, peeled and minced
- ¾ pound fresh mushrooms, trimmed and chopped
- ¼ cup chopped fresh parsley
- 4 teaspoons salt
- 2 bay leaves
- 2 tablespoons oregano
- 1 teaspoon black pepper
- ¼ cup packed brown sugar

METHOD

Place the tomatoes in a large saucepan and boil for 25 minutes, uncovered. Allow the tomatoes to cool slightly, then run them through a food mill or sieve to remove the skins and seeds.

In a large skillet, heat the olive oil and sauté the celery, onions, garlic, and mushrooms until tender. Place the sautéed vegetables in a stockpot, add the tomatoes and the remaining ingredients, and bring to a boil. Lower the heat and simmer the sauce, uncovered, until the volume has been reduced by half. (Stir frequently to prevent the sauce from burning.) Ladle into jars.

Blackened Tomato Sauce

Blackened tomatoes have been fantastically popular in gourmet cooking for the past several years. You'll understand why when you savor this smoky sauce.

YIELD: **7 half-pints**

PACK: **Hot**

HEADSPACE: **½ inch**

DIAL-GAUGE CANNER
 TIME & PRESSURE: **35 minutes/11 pounds**

WEIGHTED-GAUGE CANNER
 TIME & PRESSURE: **35 minutes/10 pounds**

INGREDIENTS

- 12 tomatoes
- 1½ cups peeled, chopped onions
- 3 garlic cloves, peeled and minced
- ¼ cup lemon juice
- ¼ cup vegetable oil
- 2 teaspoons chili powder
- 3 green chili peppers, seeded and chopped
- 2 sweet green peppers, seeded and chopped
- ½ cup chopped, loosely packed fresh cilantro

METHOD

To blacken the tomatoes, preheat a heavy-bottomed skillet until it is very hot. Turn the heat down to medium, place the unpeeled tomatoes in the skillet, and turn them frequently to blacken the skin on all sides. Remove the tomatoes from the pan, let them cool, then peel, core, and chop them, removing as many seeds as possible.

Using a blender, puree the tomatoes, onion, garlic, lemon juice, oil, and chili powder. Pour the puree into a large saucepan and add the peppers and cilantro. Bring to a boil, lower the heat, and simmer until the peppers are soft and the sauce has thickened. Ladle into jars.

Island Simmer Sauce

A fine sweet-and-sour sauce for Asian foods, this thick and delicious concoction can be made with ingredients straight from your grocery store.

YIELD: **6 pints**
PACK: **Hot**
HEADSPACE: **1 inch**
PROCESSING TIME: **20 minutes**

INGREDIENTS

    53   ounces drained, chopped canned peaches
    30   ounces crushed pineapple in juice
     1   cup chopped, pickled jalapeño peppers
     4   cups cider vinegar
    4½   tablespoons salt
    1½   cups dried chopped onions
     2   tablespoons ginger
     1   tablespoon garlic
     4   cups sugar
    1½   cups water
     ¼   cup soy sauce
     1   cup seeded, chopped red bell pepper

METHOD

Combine all the ingredients in a large stockpot and bring to a boil. Lower the heat and simmer until thick. Ladle into jars.

Georgia's Barbecue Sauce

Georgia, who has lived in North Carolina for the better part of her life, knows good barbecue sauce. This family recipe, which she was kind enough to share with us, is incontrovertible proof.

YIELD: **7 pints**
PACK: **Hot**
HEADSPACE: **1 inch**
DIAL-GAUGE CANNER
    TIME & PRESSURE: **20 minutes/11 pounds**
WEIGHTED-GAUGE CANNER
    TIME & PRESSURE: **20 minutes/10 pounds**

INGREDIENTS

     1   cup peeled, chopped onions
     ¾   cup chopped celery
     1   tablespoon salt
     1   teaspoon pepper
     3   tablespoons paprika
     2   tablespoons prepared mustard
     3   tablespoons Worcestershire sauce
     2   cups tomato paste
     2   cups prepared catsup
     1   quart water
     ¾   cup distilled white vinegar
     2   cups packed brown sugar

METHOD

Combine all the ingredients in a stockpot and bring to a boil. Lower the heat and simmer for about 30 minutes, stirring constantly. Ladle into jars when thick.

Sugarless Barbecue Sauce

Sweetened and thickened with fruit juice instead of sugar, this sauce adds zip to all barbecued meat and poultry dishes.

YIELD: **7 pints**
PACK: **Hot**
HEADSPACE: **1 inch**
DIAL-GAUGE CANNER
    TIME & PRESSURE: **35 minutes/11 pounds**
WEIGHTED-GAUGE CANNER
    TIME & PRESSURE: **35 minutes/10 pounds**

INGREDIENTS

    20   cups cored, chopped tomatoes
    1½   cups seeded, chopped sweet green peppers
    2½   cups peeled, chopped onions
     4   garlic cloves, peeled and chopped
     1   tablespoon dry mustard
     1   tablespoon paprika
     2   teaspoons salt
    3¾   cups white grape juice
    10   tablespoons lemon juice
     ½   teaspoon cayenne pepper

METHOD

Combine all the ingredients in a large stockpot. Bring to a boil, lower the heat, and simmer for about 30 minutes or until thick. Allow the mixture to cool, then run it through a food mill or sieve to remove seeds and skins. Reheat to boiling before ladling into jars.

WHETHER YOU SPOON THEM FROM ELEGANT CHINA or slurp them from favorite mugs, soups comprise the one category of home-canned food that no one should miss out on making. They're easy to prepare, fun to invent, and incredibly satisfying to serve and eat.

The recipes in this section cover a broad range of vegetable soups, from light and refreshing first courses to hearty main meals. They're all accompanied by processing instructions, of course, and you know by now that you must follow these instructions to the letter!

Recipe Tips

■ When you make up a soup recipe of your own, you'll need to look up the correct processing time and pressure for the lowest-acid ingredient and process the soup accordingly. If the chart on pages 123–26 doesn't include the ingredient you're looking for, consult your local Cooperative Extension Service agent.

■ Pressure canning will make most soup ingredients very soft in texture. To add a bit of crunchiness to any soup, just add some fresh vegetables as you heat the soup up, after you've opened the processed jar.

■ Unless the soup you've prepared is a puree, fill about half of each jar with solids as you pack it, then add liquid until there's 1 inch of headspace left.

■ Some recipes recommend running hot soup through a blender. Work in small batches when you do this, filling the blender only three-quarters of the way full and placing a clean, damp cloth over the blender lid. These precautionary steps will help prevent hot ingredients from spurting out and scalding you.

Asparagus-Leek Soup

Patti Hill, who shared this recipe with us, prepares this superb soup using the tougher stem portions of her asparagus. She freezes the tender tips and cooks them in the soup before serving it.

YIELD: **7 quarts**

PACK: **Hot**

HEADSPACE: **1 inch**

DIAL-GAUGE CANNER
TIME & PRESSURE: **40 minutes/11 pounds**

WEIGHTED-GAUGE CANNER
TIME & PRESSURE: **40 minutes/10 pounds**

INGREDIENTS

  5 cups sliced leeks

  ½ cup margarine

  ½ cup flour

  7 pounds asparagus stems

  1 gallon water

 17 vegetable or chicken bouillon cubes

 2½ teaspoons mixed spices*

 1½ teaspoons white pepper

Use any salty, commercial seasoning mixture, such as Spike.

METHOD

In a large stockpot, sauté the leeks in margarine until tender. Stir in the flour and cook 5 more minutes. Then add the asparagus stems, water, bouillon cubes, mixed spices, and pepper, and bring to a boil. Boil until the vegetables are very soft, stirring frequently.

Allow the soup to cool somewhat, puree it in a food mill or blender (see "Recipe Tips" above) and return the puree to the stockpot. Boil for 5 more minutes before ladling into jars.

Cuban Black Bean Soup with Oranges

This hearty, nutritious soup, which can also be served over rice, will satisfy even the largest of appetites.

YIELD: **7 quarts**

PACK: **Hot**

HEADSPACE: **1 inch**

DIAL-GAUGE CANNER
TIME & PRESSURE: **90 minutes/11 pounds**

WEIGHTED-GAUGE CANNER
TIME & PRESSURE: **90 minutes/10 pounds**

INGREDIENTS

  5 cups dried black beans

     Water to cover beans

 20 cups water

  5 oranges, peeled, membranes removed, seeded, and chopped

     Juice of two lemons

  3 onions, peeled and chopped

  1 tablespoon thyme

  6 bay leaves

 10 garlic cloves, peeled and chopped

     Salt and pepper to taste

METHOD

Place the black beans in a large stockpot, cover with water, and let stand overnight. Drain and then combine with 20 cups of water and the remaining ingredients. Simmer until the beans are soft, stirring occasionally. Boil hard for 5 minutes before ladling into jars.

Cucumber Soup

From the kitchen of Patti Hill, this delicious soup may be served hot or cold. For a richer consistency and more elegant presentation, heat with half-and-half or milk before serving and garnish with dill or chives.

YIELD: **7 quarts**

PACK: **Hot**

HEADSPACE: **1 inch**

DIAL-GAUGE CANNER
  TIME & PRESSURE: **40 minutes/11 pounds**

WEIGHTED-GAUGE CANNER
  TIME & PRESSURE: **40 minutes/10 pounds**

INGREDIENTS

  3 medium onions, peeled and cut into chunks

  ¼ pound margarine

  9 pounds cucumbers, peeled, seeded and cut into chunks

  2 quarts water

  6 chicken bouillon cubes

  2 teaspoons poultry seasoning

  2 teaspoons creole seasoning mix (see page 100)

  2 teaspoons mixed spices*

  ½ teaspoon white pepper

  2 teaspoons dill weed

* Use any salty, commercial seasoning mixture, such as Spike.

METHOD

Sauté the onion in the margarine until soft. Add the remaining ingredients, then cover and simmer until very soft. Process the soup in a blender (see "Recipe Tips" on the opposite page).

Return the puree to the stockpot and bring to a boil. Cook for 5 minutes before ladling into jars.

Lynn's Tomato-Bean Soup

When winter winds howl outdoors, warm your guests and family with generous servings of this rich, dark, and luscious soup.

YIELD: **6 quarts**

PACK: **Hot**

HEADSPACE: **1 inch**

DIAL-GAUGE CANNER
  TIME & PRESSURE: **90 minutes/11 pounds**

WEIGHTED-GAUGE CANNER
  TIME & PRESSURE: **90 minutes/10 pounds**

INGREDIENTS

  1 pound black beans

  1 pound lentils

  1 cup olive oil

  2 teaspoons salt

  5 onions, peeled and chopped

20 pounds tomatoes, peeled and cored

  1 cup distilled white vinegar

  ¾ cup sugar

1½ tablespoons creole seasoning mix (see page 100)

METHOD

Place the black beans and lentils in separate saucepans, cover with water, and soak overnight. To each pan, add ¼ cup olive oil and 1 teaspoon of salt and boil until soft. (The black beans will take about 30 minutes and the lentils about 15.)

In a stockpot, sauté the onions in the remaining olive oil. Add the tomatoes and cook until soft. Then blend this mixture with a hand-mixer in order to break up the tomatoes.

Drain and rinse the black beans and add them to the tomato mixture. Don't drain the lentils; just add them to the stockpot along with their liquid. Add the vinegar, sugar, and creole seasoning mix. Bring to a boil and cook for 5 minutes before ladling into jars.

Cajun Tomato Soup

Before she retired, Patti Hill used to serve this outstanding soup at her restaurant in New Orleans. Make several batches—a few for yourself and more for guests.

YIELD: **7 quarts**

PACK: **Hot**

HEADSPACE: **1 inch**

DIAL-GAUGE CANNER
TIME & PRESSURE: **40 minutes/11 pounds**

WEIGHTED-GAUGE CANNER
TIME & PRESSURE: **40 minutes/10 pounds**

INGREDIENTS

12 pounds tomatoes, peeled, cored, and chopped

9 sprigs parsley, stems removed

5 onions, peeled and cut into eighths

2 stalks celery, cut into 2-inch pieces

9 bay leaves

8 garlic cloves, peeled and cut into chunks

¼ pound margarine

2 tablespoons creole seasoning mix (see page 100)

2 tablespoons mixed spices*

1 cup packed brown sugar

1½ cups flour

1½ cups water

Use any salty, commercial seasoning mixture, such as Spike.

METHOD

Combine the first six ingredients in a very large stockpot and cook until all the vegetables are very soft. Working in batches, puree the cooked mixture in a blender (see "Recipe Tips" on page 96). To remove seeds and skins, run each blended batch through a food mill, too.

Return the puree to the stockpot and add the margarine, creole seasoning mix, mixed spices, and brown sugar. In a small bowl, whisk together the flour and water to make a thin paste. Add the paste slowly to the stockpot contents, stirring with the whisk as you do. Bring the soup to a boil and cook until it thickens. Ladle into jars.

Indian Split-Pea Soup

Serve this exquisitely flavored soup as a meal in itself or as an appetizer before any meal. Dal (yellow split peas) are found in many traditional Indian recipes.

YIELD: **7 quarts**

PACK: **Hot**

HEADSPACE: **1 inch**

DIAL-GAUGE CANNER
TIME & PRESSURE: **90 minutes/11 pounds**

WEIGHTED-GAUGE CANNER
TIME & PRESSURE: **90 minutes/10 pounds**

INGREDIENTS

3 pounds dried yellow split peas

5 quarts water

½ cup lime juice

3 cups peeled, chopped onions

4¼ cups peeled, sliced carrots

6 garlic cloves, peeled and minced

2 tablespoons cumin seed

2 tablespoons coriander seeds

1 tablespoon turmeric

1 teaspoon cayenne pepper

2 teaspoons salt

METHOD

In a large stockpot, bring the split peas and water to a boil. Then simmer gently, covered, for about 1 hour or until the peas are soft. Stir in the remaining ingredients and continue simmering the soup gently for 30 to 35 minutes. If the soup is too thick for your taste, simply thin it with water.

Broccoli Soup

Here's a terrific soup from our friend Barbara Applebaum. Thick and creamy but light, it makes a superb first course for any special meal.

YIELD: **7 quarts**

PACK: **Hot**

HEADSPACE: **1 inch**

DIAL-GAUGE CANNER
 TIME & PRESSURE: **40 minutes/11 pounds**

WEIGHTED-GAUGE CANNER
 TIME & PRESSURE: **40 minutes/10 pounds**

INGREDIENTS

    7 pounds broccoli (stems and florets)

    3 onions, peeled and chopped

    6 garlic cloves, peeled and chopped

    ½ cup margarine or vegetable oil (optional)

    1 cup uncooked white rice

   24 cups vegetable or chicken broth
       Tabasco sauce to taste
       Salt and pepper to taste

METHOD

Cut the broccoli florets from the stalks, then peel the stalks and slice them into 1- to 2-inch pieces. Sauté the broccoli stalks and florets, onions, and garlic in the margarine or vegetable oil. In a large saucepan, combine the sautéed vegetables with the rice and broth. Bring to a boil, lower the heat, and simmer gently until the vegetables are very soft.

Puree the soup in a blender (see "Recipe Tips" on page 96), return it to the stockpot, and add the Tabasco, salt, and pepper. Bring to a boil and cook for 5 minutes before ladling into jars.

Mixed Vegetable Soup

If the noon hours of your childhood were marked by an endless series of bland, commercially canned vegetable soups, get ready for a pleasant surprise.

YIELD: **7 quarts**

PACK: **Hot**

HEADSPACE: **1 inch**

DIAL-GAUGE CANNER
 TIME & PRESSURE: **95 minutes/11 pounds**

WEIGHTED-GAUGE CANNER
 TIME & PRESSURE: **95 minutes/10 pounds**

INGREDIENTS

   1½ quarts water or vegetable stock

   12 tomatoes, peeled, cored, and chopped

    7 potatoes, peeled and cut into chunks

    4 cups lima beans, fresh or frozen

    7 cups corn kernels, fresh or frozen

    3 cups carrots, peeled and sliced

    2 cups chopped celery

    2 cups peeled, chopped red onions

    5 crushed black peppercorns

    ½ cup minced fresh parsley

    2 bay leaves
       Salt and pepper to taste

METHOD

Combine all the ingredients in a large stockpot and bring to a boil. Cook over high heat for 5 minutes or until all the vegetables are thoroughly heated. Ladle into jars.

Curried Zucchini Soup

This wonderful recipe, from our friend Barbara, will cure even the worst case of "zucchini blues"—the dreadful depression that hits each summer when you realize that no matter how few zucchini or squash plants you grow, they'll always overproduce.

YIELD: **7 quarts**

PACK: **Hot**

HEADSPACE: **1 inch**

DIAL-GAUGE CANNER
    TIME & PRESSURE: **40 minutes/11 pounds**

WEIGHTED-GAUGE CANNER
    TIME & PRESSURE: **40 minutes/10 pounds**

INGREDIENTS

9 pounds zucchini and/or summer squash

4 cups peeled, chopped onions

4 garlic cloves, peeled and minced

½ cup margarine or vegetable oil

20 cups water, chicken broth, or vegetable broth

1 cup uncooked white rice

1½ tablespoons curry powder

Salt and pepper to taste

METHOD

Trim and discard the zucchini ends, then chop the zucchini into ½-inch pieces. In a large stockpot, sauté the zucchini, onions, and garlic in the margarine or oil until tender. Add the water or broth and bring to a boil. Add the rice and curry powder, lower the heat, and simmer uncovered until the vegetables are very soft and the rice is tender.

Puree the soup in a blender (see "Recipe Tips" on page 96), return the puree to the stockpot, and season to taste. If the soup is thicker than you'd like, just add more water to thin it. Boil for 5 minutes before ladling into jars.

Tomato-Okra Creole

This mouth-watering creole, from Patti Hill, may be served as a soup or ladled over white rice. For extra goodness, mix in some cooked chicken chunks or boiled shrimp before serving it.

YIELD: **7 quarts**

PACK: **Hot**

HEADSPACE: **1 inch**

DIAL-GAUGE CANNER
    TIME & PRESSURE: **45 minutes/11 pounds**

WEIGHTED-GAUGE CANNER
    TIME & PRESSURE: **45 minutes/10 pounds**

INGREDIENTS

½ cup flour

½ cup vegetable oil

4 medium onions, peeled and chopped

2 sweet green peppers, seeded and chopped

7 stalks celery, chopped

11 garlic cloves, peeled and chopped

3½ pounds okra, cut into ½-inch pieces

10 pounds tomatoes, peeled, cored, and chopped

¼ cup sugar

2 tablespoons creole seasoning mix*

Patti's terrific combination is so tasty that you may throw away your salt and pepper shakers once you've tried it. Here's the recipe:

Creole Seasoning Mix

26 ounces (1 box) table salt

1½ ounces black pepper

2 ounces cayenne pepper

1 ounce pure garlic powder

1 ounce chili powder

1 teaspoon thyme

1 teaspoon sweet basil

METHOD

In a Dutch oven, make a roux by browning the flour in the oil, stirring the mixture constantly until it turns golden brown. Add the onions, bell peppers, celery, and garlic, and sauté until the vegetables are wilted.

In a large stockpot, combine the sautéed vegetables with the okra, tomatoes, sugar, and creole seasoning mix. Simmer over low heat for about 30 minutes, stirring occasionally. Bring to a boil for 5 minutes before ladling into jars.

I F THE ONLY JELLIES and marmalades you've tasted have been the forgettable varieties at restaurants and grocery stores, you may be in for a shock—a pleasant one, we promise you. Exquisitely flavored and crystal clear homemade jellies are ambrosial, and homemade marmalades, chock full of fruit and peel, will take your breath away.

THE JELLING PROCESS

Making fruit spreads can be time consuming, but the basic steps are really quite simple. Jellies are made by cooking fruit juice and sugar, with or without added pectin (we'll describe pectin in a minute), until the mixture jells. Marmalades are made in a similar fashion, but they include small pieces of fruit and/or citrus peel and are usually less firm then jellies.

The jelling process depends on three factors: the temperature to which you cook the fruit mixture; the acidity strength of the combined ingredients; and the right combination of fruit juice, sugar, and pectin.

Pectin

Without pectin, jelly simply won't jell. This substance is found naturally in all fruits, but some (apples, crabapples, plums, grapes, and gooseberries) contain much more of it than others. Pectin is also manufactured and sold commercially. When you're making jelled fruit spreads (including marmalades) with high-pectin fruits, you won't need to add commercial pectin. When you're working with low-pectin fruits, including strawberries, cherries, and blueberries, you will.

Several types of commercial pectin are available, including liquid and powdered forms (these aren't interchangeable) and pectins for use with low- and no-sugar recipes. Pectin products do differ from one another in composition, so use the instructions and recipes that accompany the type you buy. Replenish your supply once a year, as commercial pectin has a short shelf life.

Acidity

The right amount of pectin won't guarantee jelling unless the acidity strength of the ingredients is also correct. If the acid strength is too low, you'll end up with sweet soup. If it's too high, your jelly will weep juice. When you're working with fruits that aren't very acidic, you'll add other acidic ingredients, such as lemon juice. Acidity strength can also be raised by using one part underripe fruit for every three parts mature fruit, as underripe fruit is more acidic and is also higher in pectin.

Sugar and Sugar Substitutes in Fruit Spreads

Sugar in fruit-spread recipes serves several functions. It helps the fruits retain their natural flavors, and it acts as a preservative, although you'll still need to process your jars in a boiling-water bath in order to prevent molds from growing in them. Sugar's most important role in jellies, marmalades, and other fruit spreads, however, is as a thickening agent.

Today's health-conscious food lovers sometimes find that traditional, sugar-laden fruit-spread recipes are much too sweet. For this reason, we've included a few recipes that make use of sweet fruit juices such as apple and white grape, that substitute corn syrup or honey for part of the sugar, and that include pectin as a thickener. We don't include gelatin-thickened recipes in this book because these products should be refrigerated rather than canned. Neither do we include noncaloric sweeteners, as we don't think they're good for you.

If you'd like to minimize the refined sugar in our other recipes, you may substitute corn syrup or a mild-flavored honey for up to one-quarter of the sugar in recipes that don't call for added pectin. In added-pectin recipes, you may substitute honey or corn syrup for up to one-half of the sugar. In either kind of recipe, too much corn syrup or honey will overwhelm the natural fruit flavor and will inhibit jelling.

Never arbitrarily reduce the amount of sugar in a fruit-spread recipe; your product may not jell properly and may also grow molds and yeasts.

Juice

Commercially canned and frozen fruit juices are low in pectin, so they can only be used in recipes thickened with added pectin. For recipes without added pectin, you must extract your own fresh juice from a high-pectin fruit.

Extracting juice isn't a huge ordeal. For each cup of juice, select ¼ pound of underripe fruit and ¾ pound of fully ripe fruit. Wash the fruit thoroughly in cold running water. If you're working with berries, remove their stems and caps. Then crush the fruit if it's soft or cut it into pieces if it's firm. Don't bother to peel or core fruits such as apples; much of the pectin you're after is in these portions.

Place the crushed or chopped fruit in a large saucepan. If the fruit is firm, cover it with water. If the fruit is soft, add only enough water to prevent scorching. Bring the fruit and water to a gentle simmer over low heat, stirring constantly. Soft fruits will need about 10 minutes of simmering and firm fruits about 20 to 30 minutes.

To separate the juice from the cooked fruit, first dampen a jelly bag and position it over a broad-mouthed pan or saucepan. Then pour the cooked fruit and liquid into the bag. Allow the juice to drain into the pan. Don't squeeze the bag, as forcing the juice through will make your jelly cloudy. If you don't have a jelly bag, use a sieve lined with several layers of cheesecloth. (If you use a fruit press for juice extraction, be sure to strain the pressed juice several times through a jelly bag or layered cheesecloth.)

MAKING JELLIES AND MARMALADES WITHOUT ADDED PECTIN

To prepare jellies without added pectin, you'll heat the extracted fruit juice, sugar, and in some cases lemon or lime juice to boiling, stirring until all the sugar has dissolved. Then you'll boil and stir the mixture until it reaches what's known as the jelling point.

How do you determine when the jelling point has been reached? Using a candy thermometer is the most reliable method. The chart that follows provides jelling-point temperatures for typical jelly recipes. Note that these temperatures differ depending on the altitude at which you're working.

Altitude in Feet	Jelling-Point Temperature	Altitude in Feet	Jelling-Point Temperature
Sea Level	220°F	5,000	211°F
1,000	218°F	6,000	209°F
2,000	216°F	7,000	207°F
3,000	214°F	8,000	205°F
4,000	212°F		

Another way to determine the jelling point at your altitude is to bring a saucepan of water to a boil, take its temperature with a candy thermometer, and add 8°F to that temperature.

Rather than using a candy thermometer, many jelly makers use what's known as the "sheet" or "spoon" test. To make this test, dip a metal spoon into the boiling mixture, lift it up and away from the steam, and turn it sideways. When the liquid mixture forms two drops that flow together or hang off the edge of the spoon, your jelly is done.

As soon as the jelling point has been reached, remove the pan from the heat and skim off and discard any foam. Ladle the jelly into sterilized jars, using a funnel and holding the ladle close to it so that bubbles don't form as you pour. Leave 1/4 inch of headspace. (Note that most jellies require only 5 minutes of heat processing if you live at sea level, so you must sterilize the canning jars before filling them. See page 30 for instructions.)

To make marmalades, you'll cook fruit, fruit juice, and sugar slowly over low heat, stirring until the sugar has dissolved. Then you'll boil the mixture over high heat until the mixture has almost jelled. In any marmalade recipe, it's wise to include some of the white portion of the rind, as this is the part of the fruit that contains most of the pectin.

Marmalades aren't always cooked to the jelling point. To test a marmalade to see whether or not it has cooked long enough, place a small amount on a plate and freeze it for 5 minutes. Then poke the marmalade with your finger. If it wrinkles—not just on its surface, but throughout—it's done.

MAKING JELLIES AND MARMALADES WITH ADDED PECTIN

Different pectin products are used differently, so always follow recipe directions carefully, adding ingredients in the recommended order. Never overcook the mixture, as the commercial pectin will break down.

HEAT PROCESSING FRUIT SPREADS

When we were growing up, homemade fruit spreads were often ladled into scalded jars and then sealed with a coating of wax or paraffin. The USDA now recommends that all fruit spreads be processed in a boiling-water bath.

After fastening the lids and screw bands in place, lower the jars into a boiling-water bath canner filled with simmering water. Add simmering water if necessary to cover the jars by at least 1 inch, bring the water to a boil, and process for the recommended length of time. Jellies usually require only 5 minutes, while other fruit spreads may require 10 or 15 minutes. Don't forget that at high altitudes, you must add 1 minute of extra processing time for each 1,000 feet above sea level.

Recipe Tips

■ Always use nonreactive utensils, bowls, saucepans, and stockpots when making fruit spreads. Metals such as cast iron will react with acidic ingredients. Also make sure the saucepans or stockpots you use are large. Sugar-filled fruit spreads expand tremendously when they're brought to a rolling boil!

■ Never try to double a recipe; prepare only one batch at a time. Jelly and many other fruit-spread recipes are written for particular jar sizes. Trying to fill and process 1-quart jars with a product made from a recipe for 1-pint jars may leave you with a spread that's too soft.

■ When you're working with recipes that don't require added pectin, remember that about one-quarter of the fruit you use should be underripe. With added-pectin recipes, use only mature fruit. You don't need the extra pectin that underripe fruit provides, and fully ripened fruit is always more flavorful.

■ The sugar content of fruit spreads makes them especially prone to scorching, so stir, stir, stir as you cook!

Spiced Apple Jelly
(No Added Pectin)

Fragrant, clear, tart, and sweet, this jelly is a much-improved version of the bland commercial varieties. You'll need about 4 pounds of apples (about one-fourth of them underripe) to supply the required 4 cups of juice.

YIELD: **4 half-pints**
HEADSPACE: **¼ inch**
PROCESSING TIME: **5 minutes**

INGREDIENTS

- 4 cups extracted apple juice
- 1 tablespoon lemon juice
- 1 tablespoon lime juice
- 3 cups sugar
- 2 cinnamon sticks, broken into pieces
- 6 whole allspice berries
- 6 whole cloves

METHOD

To extract the apple juice, first slice away the ends of the apples and cut them into chunks without peeling or coring them. Place the chunks in a saucepan and add 3 cups of water. Cover the pan and quickly bring the contents to a boil. Then turn the heat down and simmer for about 30 minutes or until the apple chunks are very soft. Place the cooked mixture in a jelly bag or a sieve lined with several layers of cheesecloth and allow the juice to drip from the pulp.

Measure 4 cups of the extracted juice into a large saucepan. Add the citrus juice and sugar, stirring well to dissolve the sugar. Tie the spices in a muslin or cheesecloth bag, add them to the mixture, and bring to a boil over high heat. Continue to boil vigorously for about 30 minutes or until the jellying point has been reached. Remove the pan from the heat, discard the spice bag, and skim off any foam. Ladle into sterilized jars.

Classic Mint Jelly

(No Added Pectin)

Lamb comes to mind, right? Broaden your horizons! Try this delectable jelly with luncheon meats, spicy cheeses, or as a topping on vanilla ice cream.

YIELD: **4 half-pints**
HEADSPACE: ¼ **inch**
PROCESSING TIME: **5 minutes**

INGREDIENTS

    4 cups extracted apple juice
    1¼ cups packed mint leaves
    1 cup boiling water
    1 tablespoon lemon juice
    1 tablespoon lime juice
    3 cups sugar
       Green food coloring (optional)

METHOD

Extract the apple juice first, using the instructions on page 102. Next, make a mint infusion by placing the mint leaves in a saucepan and covering them with 1 cup of boiling water. Place a lid on the pan and allow the mint leaves to steep for at least 1 hour. Strain the leaves from the liquid.

In a large saucepan, combine the apple, lemon, and lime juices with ½ cup of the mint infusion. Bring to a boil over high heat, then add the sugar. Bring the mixture back to a vigorous boil, stirring to dissolve the sugar, and cook to the jellying point. Skim away any foam, stir in the food coloring, and ladle the jelly into sterilized jars.

Rose Geranium Leaf Jelly

(No Added Pectin)

Rose geranium plants are probably better known for their scented leaves than they are for their flavors, but this jelly is as appetizing as the fresh leaves are aromatic.

YIELD: **4 half-pints**
HEADSPACE: ¼ **inch**
PROCESSING TIME: **5 minutes**

INGREDIENTS

    6 cups water
    2 cups fresh rose geranium leaves
    4 tart green apples, stemmed
    4 tart red apples, stemmed
    1 tablespoon lemon juice
    3 cups sugar

METHOD

Bring 4 cups of the water to a boil. Place the rose geranium leaves in a saucepan and cover them with the boiling water. Allow the leaves to steep for at least 2 hours.

To extract the apple juice for this recipe, chop the apples into chunks and combine the chunks with the remaining 2 cups of water in a large saucepan. Bring to a boil, lower the heat, and cook for 30 minutes or until the apples are mushy. Run the cooked mixture through a food mill to remove the peels and seeds.

Transfer the apple pulp to a dampened jelly bag. After picking the rose geranium leaves from the infusion, add the infusion to the jelly bag as well. Allow the combined juices to drip through the bag.

In a large saucepan, combine 4 cups of the mixed juices with the lemon juice and sugar. Stir to dissolve the sugar, bring to a boil, and boil over low heat for 30 minutes or until the jellying point has been reached. Remove the pan from the heat, skim away any foam, and ladle into sterilized jars.

Three-Paths-to-Heaven Jelly (Added Pectin)

Three delicious fruit flavors make this jelly unusually rich in flavor.

YIELD: **5 half-pints**
HEADSPACE: ¼ **inch**
PROCESSING TIME: **5 minutes**

INGREDIENTS

    ½ cup commercial apple juice
    ½ cup commercial white grape juice
    3 cups commercial cranraspberry juice
    4 tablespoons lemon juice
    1 package powdered pectin
    2½ cups sugar
    ½ cup honey

METHOD

Combine the juices and pectin in a large saucepan. Turn the heat to medium-high and stir to dissolve the pectin. When the mixture comes to a vigorous boil, stir in the sugar. When the mixture returns to a boil, time the boil for 1 minute, stirring all the while. As soon as the minute is up, remove the pan from the heat and skim away any foam before ladling the jelly into sterilized jars.

Hot and Sweet Pepper Jelly
(Added Pectin)

Those of you who like hot foods will find yourself adding this spicy sweet jelly to everything from bagels with cream cheese to meat and cheese dishes. If you'd like to tone down its kick, use only one jalapeño—or add one sweet pepper and leave out the jalapeños completely.

YIELD: **6 half-pints**
HEADSPACE: **¼ inch**
PROCESSING TIME: **5 minutes**

INGREDIENTS

1½ cups extracted apple juice

7 sweet green peppers, seeded

2 jalapeño peppers, seeded

1½ cups distilled white vinegar

1 tablespoon lemon juice

½ teaspoon salt

1 package powdered pectin

5 cups sugar

Green food coloring (optional)

METHOD

To extract the apple juice, follow the instructions on page 102.

Cut the sweet and hot peppers into ½-inch pieces. Using a blender, puree the peppers and vinegar. Combine the puree with the apple juice in a large mixing bowl. Cover the bowl with plastic wrap and refrigerate for 8 to 10 hours.

Strain the pepper mixture through a jelly bag or several layers of cheesecloth. Then measure 4 cups of the juice into a large saucepan.

(If you run short on juice, just add water.) Add the salt and pectin and stir well.

Bring the mixture to a vigorous boil over high heat, stirring constantly. Add the sugar, and as soon as the mixture returns to a rolling boil, time the boil for 1 minute, stirring all the while. As soon as the minute is up, remove the pan from the heat and skim away any foam. Stir in a few drops of green food coloring if you like and ladle into sterilized jars.

Quince and Cranberry Jelly
(No Added Pectin)

One version of this recipe, popular during the 1930s and 1940s, was named Paradise Jelly because the quince was once thought to be the original apple in the garden of Eden. There's no doubt that this jelly is sinfully delicious.

YIELD: **2 half-pints**
HEADSPACE: **¼ inch**
PROCESSING TIME: **5 minutes**

INGREDIENTS

2 pounds ripe quinces, peeled and cored

¾ pound tart green apples

1½ cups fresh cranberries

4 cups water

Sugar (see "Method")

METHOD

Cut the quinces and apples into chunks; don't peel or core the apples. Place the cut fruit, cranberries, and water in a large saucepan and cover the pan with a lid. Bring the fruit and liquid to a boil over high heat and continue to boil for 30 minutes or until all the fruit is very soft.

When the mixture is cool enough to handle, use a jelly bag or several layers of cheesecloth to strain the juice from it. Measure the juice into a large saucepan and add ¾ cup of sugar for each cup of juice. Stir to dissolve the sugar; then bring the mixture to a boil over high heat. Boil for 10 minutes or until the jellying point has been reached. Skim off any foam and ladle into sterilized jars.

Citrus Jelly with Ginger and Honey
(Added Pectin)

This fascinating lemon and lime jelly, flecked with bits of ginger, is made with honey instead of sugar. The added pectin serves as a thickener.

YIELD: **4 half-pints**
HEADSPACE: ¹/₄ **inch**
PROCESSING TIME: **5 minutes**

INGREDIENTS

- ½ cup lemon juice
- ¼ cup lime juice
- 2¼ cups honey
- 3 tablespoons minced, crystallized ginger
- 3 ounces commercial liquid pectin

METHOD

Combine the juices and honey in a large saucepan and bring to a boil over high heat. Add the ginger, stir to mix, and bring the mixture back to a vigorous boil. Stir in the pectin at this point, and as soon as the mixture has returned to a rolling boil, time the boil for exactly 1 minute. Remove the saucepan from the heat promptly and stir for a couple of minutes to distribute the ginger before ladling into sterilized jars.

Savory Wine Jelly
(Added Pectin)

Many wine-jelly recipes call for robust wines, such as sangria or port. In this recipe, however, we use a dry white wine, as the herb flavor can be quite fragile. Use any herb you like. Tarragon, savory, basil, and rosemary all taste delicious.

YIELD: **5 half-pints**
HEADSPACE: ¹/₄ **inch**
PROCESSING TIME: **5 minutes**

INGREDIENTS

- 2 cups plus 2 tablespoons dry white wine
- 2 tablespoons dry herbs
- 3 cups sugar
- 3 tablespoons lemon juice
- 3 ounces liquid pectin
- 5 fresh herb sprigs

METHOD

Start by making an herb-flavored wine infusion. Place 1 cup of the wine in a saucepan and quickly bring it to a full boil. Remove the pan from the heat, add the dried herbs, cover the pan, and allow the herbs to steep for 2 hours.

Strain the herbs from the liquid and pour the liquid into a 2-cup measuring cup. Add enough remaining wine to make 2 cups and pour into a large saucepan. Add the sugar and lemon juice and bring to a boil, stirring constantly. Turn up the heat and boil vigorously for 1 minute. Remove the pan from the heat and add the pectin right away, stirring to dissolve it. Skim away any foam. Place an herb sprig in each sterilized jar and then ladle in the liquid.

This jelly will take at least a week to set, so don't give the jars away too quickly!

Mixed Herb Jelly

(Added Pectin)

Not all jellies go with peanut butter! This savory jelly, for example, is delicious with meats. By varying the herb combinations, you can build an entire culinary collection.

YIELD: **3 half-pints**
HEADSPACE: **¼ inch**
PROCESSING TIME: **5 minutes**

INGREDIENTS

- ¼ cup dry or 1½ cups fresh, crushed herbs
- 3½ cups sugar
- ¼ cup distilled white vinegar
- 1 tablespoon lemon juice
- ½ package liquid pectin

METHOD

To prepare an herb infusion, select any combination of leafy herbs. Oregano, basil, thyme, marjoram, tarragon, and mint work well. Measure the dry or fresh herbs into a small saucepan. Pour 2¼ cups of boiling water over the herbs, place the lid on the pan, and allow the herbs to steep for 1 hour. Then strain out the leaves and reserve the liquid.

In a large saucepan, combine 1¾ cups of the infusion with the sugar, vinegar, and lemon juice. Bring to a vigorous boil over high heat, stirring all the while. Add the liquid pectin, return to a boil, and boil vigorously for 1 minute. Remove the pan from the heat, skim away any foam, and ladle into sterilized jars.

Cherry Calvados Jelly

(Added Pectin)

A glorious treat, this jelly will draw rave reviews from anyone lucky enough to share it with you. Calvados—the famous apple brandy from Normandy—adds a truly distinctive flavor.

YIELD: **4 half-pints**
HEADSPACE: **¼ inch**
PROCESSING TIME: **5 minutes**

INGREDIENTS

- 2 pounds pitted, sour red, canned cherries
- 1 package powdered pectin
- 2½ cups sugar
- ½ cup Calvados

METHOD

Drain and reserve the juice from the cherries. In a large saucepan, combine 1½ cups of the juice and the pectin. Bring the mixture quickly to a vigorous boil. Add the sugar, stirring to dissolve, and allow the mixture to come back to a rolling boil. Maintain the boil for exactly 1 minute, stirring all the while. Remove the pan from the heat and skim any foam from the top of the mixture. Quickly add the Calvados, stirring to distribute it evenly. Ladle into sterilized jars.

Blueberry-Citrus Marmalade

(No Added Pectin)

A favorite with people who aren't all that fond of pure citrus marmalades, this spread is extremely flavorful and its color is quite amazing.

YIELD: **5 half-pints**
HEADSPACE: **¼ inch**
PROCESSING TIME: **5 minutes**

INGREDIENTS

- 1 orange
- 1 lemon
- 1½ cups water
- ¼ cup orange juice
- ¼ cup lemon juice
- 4 cups fresh blueberries
- 3 cups sugar
- ¼ teaspoon grated nutmeg
- 1 cinnamon stick, broken into pieces
- 6 whole cloves

METHOD

Peel the orange and lemon and scrape away about half of the white pith from the back of the peels. Then slice the scraped peel into fine slivers and place the slivers in a large saucepan with the water. Bring to a boil, cover, and cook vigorously for 10 to 15 minutes or until the slivers are very soft.

Remove the membranes from the peeled orange sections and add the pulp to the boiled slivers, along with the orange and lemon juice. Cook at a slow boil for an additional 15 minutes.

Add the blueberries, sugar, and nutmeg. Tie the cinnamon-stick pieces and cloves in a muslin or cheesecloth bag and add the bag to the mixture. Bring to a boil and cook, uncovered, for 20 minutes, stirring frequently to prevent sticking. The marmalade is ready to ladle into jars when the blueberry skins have broken open and the mixture is thick. Remove the spice bag before packing the sterilized jars.

Aunt Emme's Mystery Marmalade

(No Added Pectin)

The real mystery to this marmalade is how Aunt Emme came up with such an unlikely but delicious combination of ingredients.

YIELD: **7 pints**
HEADSPACE: **¼ inch**
PROCESSING TIME: **5 minutes**

INGREDIENTS

  6 tart green apples
12 medium peaches
  2 large tomatoes
  4 medium navel oranges
      Sugar (see "Method")

METHOD

Peel and core the apples; peel and pit the peaches; and peel the tomatoes. Then chop them all coarsely, either by hand or in a food processor. Remove the seeds from the oranges and grind them (peels included) in a blender or food processor.

Combine all the fruits in a large saucepan, measuring them as you do. Bring to a boil and cook over medium heat for 10 to 12 minutes, stirring frequently. Add ¾ cup of sugar for every 1 cup of fruit. Simmer the mixture over low heat until thick, then ladle into sterilized jars.

Spiced Sour Cherry and Orange Marmalade

(No Added Pectin)

If you live in an area where cherries are grown and don't mind climbing ladders, by all means pick your own fruit. You may find fresh sour cherries at your grocery store but if you don't, canned or frozen cherries will work. Just be sure to drain them well.

YIELD: **4 half-pints**
HEADSPACE: **¼ inch**
PROCESSING TIME: **15 minutes**

INGREDIENTS

  1 large orange, quartered and seeded
  5 whole cloves
  5 allspice berries
  4 cups pitted sour cherries
  3 tablespoons lemon juice
3½ cups sugar

METHOD

Chop the orange flesh and peel coarsely and place in a large saucepan. Cover with water and bring to a boil over high heat. Boil until the orange pieces are very soft, then allow them to cool.

Tie the cloves and allspice in a cheesecloth or muslin bag and place the bag in the saucepan with the orange. Add the cherries, lemon juice, and sugar. Bring the mixture to a boil over medium heat, stirring frequently to dissolve the sugar. Turn the heat up and cook rapidly for about 35 minutes, stirring often. When the marmalade passes the "wrinkle" test (see page 103), remove the spice bag and ladle into jars.

Concord-Cranberry Marmalade
(No Added Pectin)

Here's a tart marmalade for taste buds that love to be stimulated. You must extract your own juice, so be sure to stock up on Concord grapes.

YIELD: **4 half-pints**
HEADSPACE: **¼ inch**
PROCESSING TIME: **15 minutes**

INGREDIENTS

2 cups extracted Concord grape juice

3 tablespoons grated orange peel

2 cups fresh cranberries, stems removed

3 cups sugar

METHOD

To extract the juice from the grapes, first review the instructions on pages 102–103. Then place the whole grapes in a saucepan and cover with boiling water. Simmer slowly for about 10 minutes or until the skins have broken and the fruit is very soft. Use a jelly bag or several layers of cheesecloth to strain out the juice. Refrigerate the juice for a day or two, then carefully pour off the clear juice, discarding the sediment at the bottom.

In a saucepan, combine the juice, grated orange peel, and cranberries, and bring to a boil over high heat. Turn down the heat, add the sugar, and bring the mixture slowly back to a boil, stirring constantly to dissolve the sugar. Turn the heat back up and cook for about 5 minutes or until the jellying point has been reached. (You'll need to stir the mixture gently as it boils.) Ladle into jars.

Almost Traditional Marmalade
(No Added Pectin)

The "real thing" is made with sugar, but this marmalade is made with honey. Its nearly bitter flavor is that of a truly traditional marmalade.

YIELD: **5 half-pints**
HEADSPACE: **¼ inch**
PROCESSING TIME: **10 minutes**

INGREDIENTS

2 lemons

5 oranges

12 cups water

¼ cinnamon stick, broken into pieces

1½ cups honey

1½ cups light corn syrup

METHOD

Place the whole fruits and water in a saucepan. Tie the cinnamon-stick pieces in a muslin or cheesecloth bag and place in the saucepan as well. Cover and bring the contents to a boil over high heat. Then turn the heat down and simmer very slowly for 1½ to 2 hours. Remove and discard the spice bag.

Remove the fruits, quarter them, discard the seeds, and chop. (A food processor will save time here.) Place the chopped fruit back in the liquid and bring the mixture to a boil over high heat. Stir in the honey and corn syrup and bring the mixture back to a vigorous boil, stirring constantly. Continue to boil for 20 to 30 minutes, stirring all the while, until the mixture is thick and syrupy. Then ladle into jars.

jams, preserves, and conserves

ET'S START BY DEFINING these three types of fruit spreads. Jams are thick fruit-filled spreads. They're made by crushing or chopping fruits, mixing them with sugar, and cooking them rapidly until the mixture rounds up in a spoon. Conserves are much like jams, but contain two or more types of fruit. Traditionally prepared conserves also include citrus fruits, raisins, coconut, or nuts. Preserves are whole fruits or large pieces of fruit that have been cooked until they're soft and that come in a thick, clear, almost jellylike syrup.

MAKING JAMS AND CONSERVES

To make jams and conserves, you'll peel and core the fruit, removing pits from fruits such as peaches, and removing stems and blossoms from fruits such as strawberries. Next, you'll prepare firm fruit by chopping it into small pieces and soft fruit by crushing it. (Never puree fruits for jams or you'll end up with too much liquid.)

Next, you'll combine the fruit, sugar, and other ingredients in a heavy-bottomed saucepan, heat the mixture to boiling, and cook it, while stirring constantly, until it thickens. Then you'll skim away any foam and ladle the hot jam or conserve into jars for heat processing.

A properly thickened jam or conserve will round up in a spoon when it's hot. Another way to test it is to place about ½ teaspoon onto a small plate and put the plate in the freezer. Check the consistency in a few minutes; the spread is ready to ladle into jars if it has jelled.

MAKING PRESERVES

Making preserves is somewhat similar to making jams, but unless the pieces of fruit are very large, you won't cut them into pieces. You won't cook the fruit-and-syrup combination as long either.

Recipe Tips

■ Always use nonreactive utensils, bowls, saucepans, and stockpots when making fruit spreads. Metals such as cast iron will react with acidic ingredients. Also make sure the saucepans or stockpots you use are large. Sugar-filled fruit spreads expand tremendously when they're brought to a rolling boil!

■ Never try to double a recipe; prepare only one batch at a time. Many fruit-spread recipes are written for particular jar sizes. Trying to fill and process 1-quart jars with a product made from a recipe for 1-pint jars may leave you with a spread that's too soft.

■ The sugar content of fruit spreads makes them especially prone to scorching, so stir frequently as you cook!

Gingered Pear Jam

White bread is a dietary luxury we afford ourselves only rarely. When we have it, we toast thick slabs, butter them liberally, and spread them with a thin but luscious coat of this delicately spiced jam.

YIELD: **5 half-pints**
HEADSPACE: **¼ inch**
PROCESSING TIME: **5 minutes**

INGREDIENTS

  4 pounds pears
  1 pound underripe red apples
  2 cups sugar
  2 tablespoons minced, crystallized ginger
  1 tablespoon grated lemon peel
  1 tablespoon grated orange peel
  ¼ cup lemon juice
  1 vanilla bean, split and scraped
  1 cinnamon stick, broken into pieces

METHOD

Peel, core, and chop the pears and apples. Combine the fruit, sugar, ginger, citrus peel, lemon juice, and vanilla bean in a large mixing bowl, and toss the fruit well to coat it. Cover the bowl and allow the mixture to stand at room temperature for 4 to 5 hours.

Tie the cinnamon-stick pieces in a muslin or cheese-cloth bag and place the bag in a large saucepan. Add the pear mixture and bring to a boil. Turn the heat down and simmer over low heat, stirring frequently, for 1½ hours or until the fruit is soft but still chunky. The jam should be thick at this point. Discard the vanilla bean and spice bag and ladle the hot jam into sterilized jars.

Very Berry Jam

Select your favorite berries and combine them in any proportions you like. Gooseberries, boysenberries, blueberries, blackberries, loganberries, raspberries, and dewberries are all suitable for this recipe.

YIELD: **3 pints**
HEADSPACE: **¼ inch**
PROCESSING TIME: **15 minutes**

INGREDIENTS

9 cups berries
6 cups sugar
¼ teaspoon cloves
¼ teaspoon cinnamon
¼ cup lemon juice

METHOD

Crush the berries and place them in a large saucepan. Add the sugar, spices, and lemon juice, and stir to dissolve the sugar. Bring the mixture to a boil over medium heat, stirring frequently. Continue to cook over medium heat for 30 minutes or until the mixture thickens, stirring frequently to prevent sticking. Ladle into jars.

Carrot and Bourbon Jam

The touch of alcohol in this unusual jam lends it a slightly exotic flavor and makes it the perfect holiday gift.

YIELD: **3 half-pints**
HEADSPACE: **¼ inch**
PROCESSING TIME: **10 minutes**

INGREDIENTS

10 whole cloves
4 whole allspice berries
1 cinnamon stick, broken into pieces
4 cups grated carrots
⅔ cup lemon juice
⅓ cup grated lemon peel
3 cups sugar
2 tablespoons bourbon

METHOD

Tie the spices in a muslin or cheesecloth bag and place the bag in a large saucepan. Add the carrots, lemon juice, lemon peel, and sugar. Slowly bring the mixture to a boil, stirring to dissolve the sugar. Turn the heat to low and simmer until the jam is thick. Remove from the heat and discard the spice bag. Stir in the bourbon before ladling into jars.

Sweet-and-Savory Tomato Jam

Tangy but sweet, this wonderful jam complements an amazing array of foods, from cheeses and savory breads to meat dishes. Let the sealed jars age for a week or two before opening them.

YIELD: **4 half-pints**
HEADSPACE: **¼ inch**
PROCESSING TIME: **5 minutes**

INGREDIENTS

8 pounds tomatoes
1 teaspoon salt
2 tablespoons granulated sugar
¼ cup packed brown sugar
¼ cup distilled white vinegar
½ teaspoon black pepper
½ teaspoon cinnamon
½ teaspoon cloves

METHOD

Peel and core the tomatoes, then cut them into chunks. In a large saucepan, combine the tomatoes, salt, and granulated sugar, stirring well to blend. Bring to a boil over high heat. Then cook over medium heat, uncovered, for 35 to 40 minutes, stirring frequently. When the tomatoes have reduced and thickened, add the remaining ingredients and continue to cook until the jam is the desired consistency. This will take another 35 to 40 minutes. Ladle into sterilized jars.

Cherry-Orange Conserve

This conserve is an outstanding example of one that can be made with honey instead of sugar. Be sure to select a mild-flavored honey, or you'll drown out the flavors of the other ingredients.

YIELD: **3 half-pints**
HEADSPACE: **¼ inch**
PROCESSING TIME: **15 minutes**

INGREDIENTS

  2 oranges
  1 tablespoon grated
     orange peel
  4 cups sweet or sour cherries
  ½ cup lemon juice
  1 tablespoon grated
     lemon peel
  ½ cup honey
  ½ teaspoon salt
  1 cinnamon stick, broken
     into pieces
  8 whole cloves

METHOD

Peel and seed the oranges. Remove the membranes from the orange sections and cut the flesh into ½-inch cubes. In a large saucepan, combine the orange pieces, grated orange peel, cherries, lemon juice, lemon peel, honey, and salt. Tie the whole spices in a muslin or cheesecloth bag and place the bag in the saucepan. Bring the mixture to a boil over high heat. Then turn the heat down and simmer the mixture very gently for about 25 minutes. Remove the spice bag and thicken the mixture by bringing it back to a vigorous boil for 5 minutes. Ladle into jars.

Pear and Apple Conserve with Almonds

A traditional conserve, complete with nuts, this delicious spread can be made even more flavorful by stirring in a dash of rum before ladling it into jars.

YIELD: **4 half-pints**
HEADSPACE: **¼ inch**
PROCESSING TIME: **10 minutes**

INGREDIENTS

  1 pound peeled, cored pears
  1 pound peeled, cored
     apples
  3 tablespoons lemon juice
1¼ cups water
  1 tablespoon peeled, minced
     gingerroot
  5 cups sugar
  3 ounces peeled, blanched,
     chopped almonds

METHOD

Cut the pears and apples into ½-inch cubes and place them in a saucepan with the lemon juice, water, and ginger. Bring the mixture to a boil over high heat and boil for about 5 or 10 minutes or until the fruit is soft.

Add the sugar and stir to dissolve. Then boil vigorously for 15 minutes or until the syrup has thickened considerably. Don't forget to stir! Remove the pan from the heat, stir in the almonds, and ladle the conserve into jars.

Honeydew-Peach Conserve

The cashews in this conserve lend it a wonderfully robust texture, one that complements the more delicate flavors of the fruits. Like any conserve, this makes a delicious dessert sauce, too.

YIELD: **4 half-pints**
HEADSPACE: **¼ inch**
PROCESSING TIME: **10 minutes**

INGREDIENTS

3½ cups peeled, pitted, and
     chopped underripe peaches
  3 tablespoons grated
     orange peel
  1 tablespoon grated
     lemon peel
  ½ cup orange juice
  5 cups peeled, seeded,
     chopped honeydew melon
  3 cups sugar
  ½ cup chopped cashews

METHOD

Combine the peaches, grated citrus peel, and orange juice in a large saucepan. Bring to a boil over high heat, stirring frequently. Turn down the heat, cover, and cook slowly for 10 minutes or until the fruit is soft. Stir the mixture occasionally as it cooks.

Remove the pan from the heat. Add the melon, sugar, and cashews, and return to a boil. Continue to cook for 10 minutes, stirring constantly. Remove the pan from the heat again. To thicken the juice, you must cook it separately. Using a colander, drain the juice from the fruit, return the juice to the pan, and boil vigorously for about 10 minutes or until the juice has reduced by half. Add the cooked fruit, reheat to boiling, and ladle into jars.

Green Tomato Conserve

Take the label off the jar and serve this tantalizingly tart conserve to folks who say they don't like green tomatoes. You won't lose any friends!

YIELD: **7 pints**
HEADSPACE: **¼ inch**
PROCESSING TIME: **10 minutes**

INGREDIENTS

- 1 lemon
- 1 lime
- 1½ cups water
- 16 green tomatoes
- 1 cinnamon stick, broken into pieces
- 2 tablespoons mixed pickling spices
- 2 cups peeled, cored, and chopped tart green apples
- 3 cups sugar

METHOD

Peel the lemon and lime and set the fruit aside. Slice the peels into slivers, place in a large saucepan, and add the water. Bring to a boil, lower the heat, and simmer for 30 minutes or until the peels are tender.

While the peels are cooking, parboil the green tomatoes for 5 minutes and then chop them into small chunks. Tie the cinnamon-stick pieces and pickling spices in a muslin or cheesecloth bag.

Add the chopped tomatoes, spice bag, apples, and sugar to the cooked citrus peel and return to a boil. Boil for 15 minutes, stirring constantly. Remove the spice bag, reduce the heat, and simmer for 20 minutes.

As the mixture is simmering, cut the lemon and lime into thin slices, discarding the seeds. Add the slices to the simmering mixture and continue to cook for another 20 minutes, stirring frequently. Ladle into jars.

Island Conserve

If you're already a dreamer, this conserve is for you. If you're not, just close your eyes, take a taste, and before you know it, you'll be drifting off to tropical climes.

YIELD: **7 half-pints**
HEADSPACE: **¼ inch**
PROCESSING TIME: **10 minutes**

INGREDIENTS

- 3 small papayas, peeled and seeded
- 1 cup plus 2 tablespoons canned or fresh crushed pineapple, drained
- 2 tablespoons lemon juice
- 2 tablespoons lime juice
- 1 tablespoon grated lemon peel
- 5½ cups sugar
- 1 teaspoon peeled, minced gingerroot
- 1¼ cups golden raisins

METHOD

Cut the papayas into ½-inch pieces and combine with the pineapple, citrus juices, lemon peel, and 1¼ cups of the sugar in a large saucepan. Bring to a boil over medium heat, stirring frequently. Add the remaining sugar and the ginger and cook until thickened, stirring constantly. Then stir in the raisins, cook for another minute or two, and ladle into jars.

Old-Fashioned Plum Preserves

Royal colors and royal flavors make this traditional preserve an all-time favorite—even with commoners.

YIELD: **4 pints**
HEADSPACE: ½ **inch**
PROCESSING TIME: **20 minutes**

INGREDIENTS

- 4 pounds ripe plums
- 2 cups water
- 1 cup granulated sugar
- ½ cup packed brown sugar
- 3 tablespoons grated orange peel
- 1 cinnamon stick, broken into pieces

METHOD

Prick the plums with a fork to keep the skins from breaking apart when the plums are cooked.

Combine the water, granulated sugar, brown sugar, and grated orange peel in a large saucepan. Tie the cinnamon-stick pieces in a muslin or cheesecloth bag and add the bag to the saucepan. Bring to a boil over medium heat, stirring until the sugar has dissolved.

Lower the heat and simmer the syrup, uncovered, for 10 minutes. Place the plums in the syrup and bring the syrup to a boil again before removing the spice bag and ladling the plums and syrup into jars.

Sweet Melon Preserves

Skip this preserve recipe only if you don't have a single sweet tooth in your head. It's thick, beautiful and—just as preserves used to be—very, very sweet.

YIELD: **4 half-pints**
HEADSPACE: ½ **inch**
PROCESSING TIME: **10 minutes**

INGREDIENTS

- 3 pounds peeled and seeded melon or cantaloupe
- 4 cups sugar
  Juice of 2 small lemons
  Grated peel of 1 lemon

METHOD

Cut the melon into ½-inch cubes. Place the cubes in a bowl and toss with the sugar. Cover the bowl and let the fruit stand at room temperature for 8 to 10 hours.

In a large saucepan, combine the melon mixture, lemon juice, and lemon peel. Bring to a boil and cook vigorously, stirring frequently, until the syrup has reduced and thickened. Ladle into jars.

Grand Marnier Preserves

We thought about calling these "Dehydrated Fruit Preserves," but that title wouldn't do justice to the remarkable blend of flavors that this very flexible recipe offers. You may use any single dried fruit or combine two or more.

YIELD: **3 half-pints**
HEADSPACE: ½ **inch**
PROCESSING TIME: **10 minutes**

INGREDIENTS

- 1 orange
- 1 lemon
- 2 cups water
- ¼ cup granulated sugar
- ¼ cup packed brown sugar
- 1 vanilla bean, split and scraped
- 12 ounces dried fruit
- ¼ teaspoon salt
- ¼ cup Grand Marnier

METHOD

Cut the orange and lemon into ¼-inch thick slices, removing the seeds as you do and discarding the ends. Mix the water, granulated sugar, and brown sugar in a large saucepan. Add the vanilla bean and bring the mixture to a boil over high heat. Turn the heat down and simmer for 5 to 10 minutes. Add the citrus slices and the dried fruit and boil over medium-low heat for about 35 minutes or until the fruit is very tender. Don't forget to stir!

Remove the pan from the heat, discard the vanilla bean, and stir in the Grand Marnier. Ladle into jars.

fruit butters, sauces, and syrups

STARTING THE MORNING with whole-grain toast is good for your body. Spreading thick, creamy, homemade fruit butter on that toast is good for your soul. And although you wouldn't want to end every day by indulging in sweet foods, once in awhile, a fine dessert drowned in delicious, homemade fruit sauce or syrup is more than justifiable.

MAKING FRUIT BUTTERS

The first step in making any fruit butter is to cook the fruit until it's soft. Then you'll either puree the fruit in a blender or food processor, or run it through a food mill or fine-meshed sieve. Next, you'll cook this puree slowly, along with sugar and spices. Constant stirring is required, as butters are especially prone to scorching and sticking. To test your cooked butter, place a spoonful onto a cool plate. If the butter leaks juice onto the plate, it's not done yet.

MAKING FRUIT SAUCES AND SYRUPS

Recipe instructions for these products vary, but in general, fruit syrups are simply combinations of fruit juice and sugar or other sweeteners. You'll just boil the ingredients to thicken them. Fruit sauces are cooked in a similar fashion, but they contain pieces of soft fruit.

Tart Cranberry Butter

*For a tongue-tingling butter—
one that's as good on turkey as it is
on bread—try this unusual recipe.*

YIELD: **6 half-pints**
HEADSPACE: **¼ inch**
PROCESSING TIME: **10 minutes**

INGREDIENTS

- ⅔ cup extracted or commercial apple juice
- 2½ pounds fresh cranberries
- 1¼ cups maple syrup
- ¼ cup honey
- 2 cinnamon sticks, broken into pieces
- 3 allspice berries
- 4 whole cloves

METHOD

To extract the apple juice, refer to the instructions on pages 102–103.

Bring the apple juice and cranberries to a boil in a large saucepan. Simmer, stirring frequently, for 25 to 30 minutes or until the cranberry skins have broken and the fruit is soft. When the mixture is cool enough to handle, puree it in a blender or run it through a food mill.

Return the puree to the saucepan and add the sweeteners. Tie the spices in a muslin or cheesecloth bag and place the bag in the saucepan. Cook over medium heat, stirring constantly, for about 20 minutes or until the mixture has thickened. Remove the spice bag before ladling into jars.

Strawberry-Pear Butter

*Jars of this butter may not survive long enough to make their way
to the breakfast table. We dare you to sample one spoonful—
and not dip in for another.*

YIELD: **3 half-pints**
HEADSPACE: **¼ inch**
PROCESSING TIME: **10 minutes**

INGREDIENTS

- 4 pounds pears, peeled, cored, and chopped
- 4 cups strawberries, hulled and sliced
- 1¼ cups water
  Sugar (see "Method")
- 1 cinnamon stick, broken into pieces
- 4 allspice berries

METHOD

Combine the pears, strawberries, and water in a large saucepan and bring to a boil over high heat. Then simmer, stirring frequently, for 1 hour or longer, until the pears are very soft and the mixture has thickened. Remove the pan from the heat.

When the mixture is cool enough to handle, run it through a food mill or use a spoon to force it through a fine-meshed plastic sieve. Return the puree to the saucepan, measuring it as you do. For each 2 cups of puree, add 1½ cups of sugar. Tie the spices in a muslin or cheesecloth bag and place the bag in the saucepan as well.

Bring the mixture to a simmer, stirring until the sugar has dissolved. Continue to simmer, over low heat, stirring frequently, for 20 to 30 minutes or until the butter is as thick as desired. Remove the spice bag and ladle the butter into jars.

Kate's Peach Butter

It's no surprise that Kate's peach butter wins awards. The color is lovely (Kate uses red peaches); the whole spices lend it an especially subtle flavor (ground spices sometimes taste overwhelming); and it's made with loving patience.

YIELD: **7 half-pints**
HEADSPACE: **¼ inch**
PROCESSING TIME: **10 minutes**

INGREDIENTS

    4 pounds peaches
    2 cups water
       Sugar (see "Method")
    1 cinnamon stick, broken
       into pieces
    6 whole cloves
    6 allspice berries
    ½ teaspoon salt (optional)

METHOD

Peel, pit, and slice the peaches. (Kate peels her peaches by placing them in boiling water for a minute and then submerging them in cold water until the peels are cool enough to slip off.) Place the sliced fruit in a large saucepan, add the water, and cook over medium heat until the peaches are very soft. When the cooked peaches have cooled, puree them in a blender or food processor.

Measure the puree back into the saucepan, adding ½ cup sugar for each cup of puree. Place the spices in a muslin or cheesecloth bag and add the bag to the saucepan, along with the salt. Cook the puree over low heat until the sugar dissolves and the puree comes to a boil. Then bring the puree to a medium boil and continue to cook, stirring constantly, for 1 to 1½ hours or until the butter is thick. Remove the spice bag and ladle into jars.

Apricot-Prune Butter

As flavorful and rich as a fruit butter can be, this one is mouth-watering when it's spread thinly on slices of whole-grain toast. It's also superb with roast poultry.

YIELD: **4 half-pints**
HEADSPACE: **¼ inch**
PROCESSING TIME: **10 minutes**

INGREDIENTS

    ½ pound pitted dried prunes
    ½ pound dried apricots
    3¼ cups water
    ¾ cup honey
    ½ cup distilled white vinegar
    ½ teaspoon grated nutmeg
    6 allspice berries
    6 whole cloves

METHOD

Rinse the prunes well under cold running water and place them, along with the apricots, in a large saucepan. Add the water and bring to a boil over high heat. Turn the heat down and simmer for about 20 minutes or until the fruit is tender. (There will still be thin liquid in the saucepan.) Remove the pan from the heat. When the fruit has cooled, drain it well.

Puree the fruit in a blender or food processor or run it through a food mill. In the empty saucepan, combine the puree with the honey, vinegar, and nutmeg. Tie the allspice berries and cloves in a muslin or cheesecloth bag and place the bag in the mixture. Bring the mixture to a simmer and cook slowly for about 15 minutes or until as thick as desired. Remove the spice bag before ladling into jars.

Carnival Apple Butter

Bring the carnival home with this caramel-flavored apple butter.

YIELD: **6 half-pints**
HEADSPACE: **¼ inch**
PROCESSING TIME: **10 minutes**

INGREDIENTS

4 pounds sweet red apples
4 pounds tart green apples
1 cup water
4 cups sugar
2 cinnamon sticks, broken into pieces
8 whole cloves
2 tablespoons peeled, minced gingerroot
2 tablespoons lemon juice

METHOD

Without peeling or coring them, cut the apples into chunks and place them in a large saucepan. Add the water and bring to a boil over high heat. Turn the heat down to medium and cook, stirring frequently, for about 30 minutes or until the apples are very soft.

When the apples are cool enough to handle, run them through a food mill to remove the peels and seeds. Then return 12 cups of the pulp to the saucepan. In a separate saucepan, heat 2 cups of the sugar over medium heat until the sugar melts and turns golden brown.

Add the caramelized sugar to the apple pulp; the caramel will harden. Add the remaining sugar as well. Tie the spices and ginger-root in a muslin or cheesecloth bag and add the bag to the mixture. Bring the mixture to a slow simmer and cook for about 1 hour or until the butter thickens, stirring often to prevent sticking. Remove the spice bag, stir in the lemon juice, and ladle into jars.

Orange-Apricot Butter

The lovely color of this butter almost matches its wonderful taste. Be sure to gift wrap a few jars for the holiday season.

YIELD: **5 half-pints**
HEADSPACE: **¼ inch**
PROCESSING TIME: **10 minutes**

INGREDIENTS

6 cups pitted, chopped apricots
½ cup water
  Maple syrup (see "Method")
½ cup frozen orange-juice concentrate
¼ teaspoon nutmeg
¼ teaspoon salt
1 cinnamon stick, broken into pieces
2 thin slices peeled gingerroot

METHOD

In a saucepan, combine the apricots and water. Bring to a boil, lower the heat, and simmer until the apricots are very soft. Remove from the heat. When the mixture is cool enough to handle, run it through a food mill to remove the peels.

Measure the puree into a large saucepan, adding ¼ cup maple syrup for each cup of puree. Then add the juice, nutmeg, and salt. Tie the cinnamon-stick pieces and ginger in a muslin or cheesecloth bag and add the bag to the mixture as well. Bring to a boil, lower the heat, and simmer, stirring constantly, until thick. Remove the spice bag before ladling into jars.

Lemon-Tomato Butter

This recipe may be stretching the concept of fruit butter to its outer limits, but it's delicious nevertheless.

YIELD: **5 half-pints**
HEADSPACE: **¼ inch**
PROCESSING TIME: **10 minutes**

INGREDIENTS

- 2 lemons, peeled, quartered, and seeded
- 14 large yellow tomatoes, cut into chunks
- 2 cups sugar
- ¼ teaspoon salt
- ½ cup honey
- ½ cup light corn syrup

METHOD

In a food processor or blender, grind the lemon quarters.

Combine the ground lemons with the tomatoes in a large saucepan and bring to a boil. Lower the heat and simmer until the tomatoes are soft. Remove from the heat. When the mixture is cool enough to handle, run it through a food mill or sieve.

Measure 9 cups of the puree into a large saucepan. Stir in the sugar, salt, honey, and corn syrup. Slowly bring to a boil, then simmer over low heat until thick enough to round up in a spoon. Stir frequently, or the butter will stick. Ladle into jars.

Brandied Fruit Sauce

Before you treat yourself to this syrup, make preparations for a pleasure-induced state somewhat akin to a coma. Sweet, sweet, sweet!

YIELD: **4 pints**
HEADSPACE: **½ inch**
PROCESSING TIME: **20 minutes**

INGREDIENTS

- 2 teaspoons butter
- 1 cup shelled hazelnuts
- 3 cups water
- 1 cup light corn syrup
- 3½ cups granulated sugar
- 1 cup packed brown sugar
  Juice of 3 oranges
  Juice of 1 lemon
- 2 tablespoons grated orange peel
- 8 ounces dried apricots, chopped
- 10 ounces dried figs, chopped
- 1 cup golden raisins, chopped
- ¾ cup brandy

METHOD

Melt the butter in a large skillet. Make sure the heat is low, add the nuts, and brown them, stirring constantly, for 2 or 3 minutes. Drain the nuts on brown paper or paper towels.

In a large saucepan, combine the water, corn syrup, granulated sugar, brown sugar, citrus juice, and orange peel. Quickly bring the mixture to a boil, stirring to dissolve the sugar. Over medium-low heat, simmer for 15 minutes or until the mixture reaches 220°F. Add the dried fruits, turn the heat to low, cover the pan, and simmer for 3 minutes. Then stir in the nuts and brandy and ladle into jars.

Praline Sauce

A superb pecan syrup for vanilla ice cream, this sauce is also delicious dribbled over pound cake.

YIELD: **8 half-pints**
HEADSPACE: **¼ inch**
PROCESSING TIME: **20 minutes**

INGREDIENTS

- 1 cup sugar
- 3 cups water
- 2½ cups light corn syrup
- ½ cup maple syrup
- ½ cup light molasses
- 3 cups pecan pieces
- ½ cup bourbon

METHOD

In a large saucepan, combine the sugar, water, corn syrup, maple syrup, and molasses. Slowly bring to a boil over medium heat, stirring constantly. Add the nuts, lower the heat, and cover the pan. Simmer, covered, for 10 minutes, stirring occasionally to prevent sticking. Remove the lid and stir in the nuts and bourbon before ladling into jars.

Spiced Apple Syrup

Try this distilled version of Mom-and-apple-pie with any fruit-based dessert. You won't be disappointed. Neither will Mom.

YIELD: **6 half-pints**
HEADSPACE: **¼ inch**
PROCESSING TIME: **10 minutes**

INGREDIENTS

6 cups extracted apple juice

2 cinnamon sticks, broken into pieces

4 allspice berries

2 thin slices peeled gingerroot

5 cups sugar

4 cups water

3 cups light corn syrup

¼ cup lemon juice

METHOD

To extract the apple juice, refer to the instructions on pages 102–103.

Tie the cinnamon-stick pieces, allspice berries, and ginger slices in a muslin or cheesecloth bag. Place the bag in a saucepan and add the apple juice. Bring to a boil, lower the heat, and simmer for 5 minutes.

In a large saucepan, combine the sugar and water and heat to 260°F. (Use a candy thermometer here.) Then add the apple juice, spice bag, and corn syrup, return to a boil, and cook over high heat for 5 minutes. Remove the spice bag and stir in the lemon juice just before ladling into jars.

Raspberry Syrup

Indulging in this exquisite dessert syrup is like drowning in melted rubies.

YIELD: **6 half-pints**
HEADSPACE: **¼ inch**
PROCESSING TIME: **20 minutes**

INGREDIENTS

8½ cups raspberries, stemmed, hulled, and crushed

¼ cup lemon juice

3¼ cups sugar

¾ cups light corn syrup

METHOD

Combine the crushed berries and lemon juice in a large saucepan. Bring to a boil, stirring frequently, and then pour the mixture through a damp-ened jelly bag. Allow the juice to drip for 3 hours.

Measure 3 to 4 cups of the juice into a large saucepan and add the sugar and corn syrup. Quickly bring to a boil, stirring constantly. Cook for 2 minutes before ladling into jars.

Grenadine

This famous syrup is the perfect flavoring for many desserts and is also used in some cocktails.

YIELD: **6 half-pints**
HEADSPACE: **¼ inch**
PROCESSING TIME: **10 minutes**

INGREDIENTS

9 pomegranates

1¾ cups sugar

¾ cup light corn syrup

METHOD

Peel the pomegranates and pull the seeds and pulp apart to release the seeds. Discard all the white pulp. Measure six cups of the red seeds and red pulp into a large bowl. Crush the seeds with a potato masher and stir in the sugar. Cover the bowl and let stand overnight.

Pour the pomegranate mixture into a large saucepan and slowly bring to a boil. Then lower the heat and simmer for 10 minutes. Pour the mixture into a dampened jelly bag to remove the inner seeds and pulp. Return the juice to the saucepan, add the corn syrup, and simmer for 10 minutes over medium heat before ladling into jars.

canning common vegetables and fruits

The chart that follows will help you prepare, pack, and process individual fruits and vegetables—
effectively and safely.

Items marked with an asterisk (*) are not recommended for canning alone, but are often pickled,
used in combined-food preparations such as soups, or—in the case of berries—used to make fruit spreads.

Food	Style of Pack	Boiling-water Bath Canning or Pressure Canning	Jar Size	Processing Time (in Minutes)	Pressure	Procedure
Apple Juice	Hot	Boiling-water bath	1/2 pint Pint Quart	5 10 10		To extract juice, see instructions on page 102. Refrigerate juice for 24 to 48 hours. Carefully pour off liquid and discard sediment. Strain liquid through layered, damp cheesecloth. Quickly bring to a boil and pack into sterilized jars, leaving 1/4-inch headspace.
Apples	Hot	Boiling-water bath	1/2 pint Pint Quart	15 20 20		Wash, peel, and core apples. Cut into pieces. To prevent darkening, place in antioxidant solution. Drain, then boil 5 minutes in syrup, juice, or water. Pack apples in jars to 1/2 inch of top. Cover with boiling syrup, juice, or water, leaving 1/2-inch headspace.
Applesauce	Hot	Boiling-water bath	1/2 pint Pint Quart	15 20 20		Make applesauce according to your recipe, and pack hot, leaving 1/2-inch headspace.
Apricots	Raw	Boiling-water bath	1/2 pint Pint Quart	20 25 30		See Peaches.
	Hot	Boiling-water bath	1/2 pint Pint Quart	15 20 25		See Peaches.
Asparagus (Preferred Method: Hot)	Hot	Pressure can	Pint Quart	30 40	10 lbs.	Wash and trim off tough skin and ends. Wash again. Cut into 1-inch pieces or leave whole. Cover with boiling water and boil 2 or 3 minutes. Add salt (1 tsp. per quart) if desired. Pack asparagus loosely and cover with boiling water, leaving 1-inch headspace.
	Raw	Pressure can	Pint Quart	30 40	10 lbs.	Wash and trim as for hot pack. Add salt to each jar if desired. Pack asparagus as tightly as possible without crushing, leaving 1-inch space at top. Cover with boiling water, leaving 1-inch headspace.
Beans, dried	Hot	Pressure can	Pint Quart	75 90	10 lbs.	Use this method for any variety of dried beans or peas. Cover with cold water. Let stand 12 to 18 hours in a cool place, then boil for 30 minutes. Pack hot into jars to within 1 inch of top. Add salt (1/2 tsp. per quart) if desired. Cover with boiling water, leaving 1-inch headspace.
Beans, fresh lima	Raw	Pressure can	Pint Quart	40 50	10 lbs.	Shell and wash. Pack small beans loosely to within 1 inch of top in pints and 1-1/2 inches in quarts. With large beans, leave 1 inch for pints and 1-1/4 inches for quarts. Add salt (1 teaspoon per quart), if desired. Cover with boiling water, leaving 1-inch headspace.
	Hot	Pressure can	Pint Quart	40 50	10 lbs.	Shell and wash. Cover with boiling water and bring to a boil. Pack beans loosely in jar to 1 inch of top. Add salt (1 tsp. per quart), if desired. Cover with boiling water, leaving 1-inch headspace.
Beans, Yellow and Green (Preferred Method: Hot)	Hot	Pressure can	Pint Quart	20 25	10 lbs.	Wash, trim ends, and leave whole or cut into 1-inch pieces. Cover with boiling water and boil 5 minutes. Pack beans in jars loosely. Add salt (1 tsp. per quart) if desired, then cover with boiling cooking liquid or boiling water, leaving 1-inch headspace.
	Raw	Pressure can	Pint Quart	20 25	10 lbs.	Prepare as for hot pack. Pack tightly in jars to 1 inch of top. Add salt (1 tsp. per quart) if desired. Cover with boiling water, leaving 1-inch headspace.
Beets, pickled	Hot	Boiling-water bath	Pint Quart	30 30		Cut off tops, leaving 1 inch of stem and root. Wash beets, cover with boiling water, and cook until tender. Remove stem, skins, and roots, then slice. For pickling syrup, combine 2 cups vinegar to 1 cup sugar and heat to boiling. Pack beets in jars to 1/2 inch of top. Cover with boiling syrup, leaving 1/2-inch headspace.
Beets, unpickled	Hot	Pressure can	Pint Quart	30 35	10 lbs.	Sort beets by size. Cut off tops, leaving 1-inch stems and roots to prevent color bleeding. Wash, boil for 20 minutes, cool, and slip off skins. Add salt (1 tsp. per quart) if desired. Skin, trim, cut, and pack into jars to 1 inch of top. (Baby beets can be left whole.) Cover with boiling water, leaving 1-inch headspace.
*Berries, soft	Raw	Boiling-water bath	Pint Quart	15 20		This method is preferred for raspberries, blackberries, boysenberries, dewberries, loganberries, or any other soft berry. Wash, cap, and stem berries, if necessary; drain well. Shaking berries down gently, fill jars to 1/2 inch of top. Cover with boiling syrup, juice, or water, leaving 1/2-inch headspace.
*Berries, firm	Hot	Boiling-water bath	Pint Quart	15 20		This method is preferred for firmer berries: blueberries, cranberries, currants, elderberries, gooseberries, and huckleberries. Wash berries thoroughly and drain well. Heat berries in boiling water for 30 seconds and drain. Pack berries and cooking liquid to 1/2 inch of top. If the berries haven't made enough of their own juice, cover them with boiling syrup or water.

Food	Style of Pack	Boiling-water Bath Canning or Pressure Canning	Jar Size	Processing Time (in Minutes)	Pressure	Procedure
*Broccoli	Hot	Pressure can	Pint Quart	30 35	10 lbs.	Cut off woody, tough stems; old leaves; and yellowing blossoms. Soak in cold, salty water for 10 to 15 minutes to drive out any clinging bugs. Rinse well and pick over. Cut into 2-inch pieces. Cover cut vegetables with boiling water and boil for 3 minutes. Drain, reserving liquid. Pack tightly. Cover with boiling liquid, leaving 1-inch headspace.
Brussels Sprouts	Hot	Pressure can	Pint Quart	30 35	10 lbs.	Choose small sprouts that will fit easily into jars. Larger sprouts that are cut in half or into wedges are more likely to fall apart during boiling. Cover sprouts with boiling water and boil for 3 minutes. Drain, reserving liquid. Pack tightly and cover with boiling liquid, leaving 1-inch headspace.
Cabbage	Hot	Pressure can	Pint Quart	30 35	10 lbs.	Clean and cut into small wedges. Cover cut wedges with boiling water and boil for 3 minutes. Drain, reserving liquid. Pack tightly and cover with boiling liquid, leaving 1-inch headspace.
Carrots (Preferred Method: Hot)	Hot	Pressure can	Pint Quart	25 30	10 lbs.	Wash and peel carrots. Slice, dice, or leave whole. Cover with boiling water, bring to a boil, and simmer for 5 minutes. Pack carrots in jars to 1 inch of top. Add salt (1 tsp. per quart) if desired. Cover with hot liquid or water, leaving 1-inch headspace.
	Raw	Pressure can	Pint Quart	25 30	10 lbs.	Wash, peel, and slice as for hot pack, then pack tightly in jars to 1 inch of top. Add salt (1 tsp. per quart) if desired. Cover with hot cooking liquid or water, leaving 1-inch headspace.
*Cauliflower	Hot	Pressure can	Pint Quart	25 30	10 lbs.	Clean and cut into small wedges. Cover wedges with boiling water and boil for 3 minutes. Drain, reserving liquid. Pack tightly and cover with boiling liquid, leaving 1-inch headspace.
*Celery	Hot	Pressure can	Pint Quart	30 35	10 lbs.	Wash and trim off tough leaves and woody bottoms. Cut into 1-inch pieces. Cover with boiling water and boil for 3 minutes. Drain, reserving liquid. Pack jars and cover with boiling liquid, leaving 1-inch headspace.
Cherries, sour and sweet	Raw	Boiling-water bath	Pint Quart	25 25		Wash, stem, and remove pits in sour or pie cherries. Sweet cherries need not be pitted, but prick them with a pin or the tip of a knife so they don't burst during processing. Fill jars to 1/2 inch of top, shaking cherries down gently. Cover with boiling juice, syrup, or water, leaving 1/2-inch headspace.
	Hot	Boiling-water bath	Pint Quart	15 20		Prepare as above. Place cherries in pan and add 1/4 cup water, juice, or syrup to each quart of drained fruit. Cover pan and bring to a boil. Pack hot, leaving 1/2-inch headspace.
Corn, cream style	Hot	Pressure can	Pint	85	10 lbs.	Husk corn, remove silk, and wash. Blanch ears 4 minutes in boiling water. Cut corn from cob at the center of the kernel, then scrape remaining corn from the cob with a table knife. Add 1 pint boiling water for each quart of corn. Heat to boiling. Add salt (1/2 tsp. per jar) if desired. Pack hot corn and liquid, leaving 1-inch headspace.
Corn, whole kernel (Preferred Method: Hot)	Hot	Pressure can	Pint Quart	55 85	10 lbs.	Husk corn, remove silk, and wash. Blanch 3 minutes in boiling water. Cut corn from cobs at about 3/4 the depth of the kernel. To each quart of kernels, add 1 cup hot water. Bring to a boil over medium heat, stirring so kernels won't scorch. Simmer 5 minutes. Add salt (1 tsp. per quart) if desired. Fill jars with corn and cooking liquid, leaving 1-inch headspace.
	Raw	Pressure can	Pint Quart	55 85	10 lbs.	Prepare as for hot pack. Fill jars with raw kernels, leaving 1 inch at top. Do not shake or press down. Add salt (1 tsp. per quart) if desired. Add fresh boiling water, leaving 1-inch headspace.
Currants	Raw	Boiling-water bath	1/2 pint Pint Quart	10 15 20		See Berries, firm.
*Eggplant	Hot	Pressure can	Pint Quart	30 40	10 lbs.	Wash and peel, then slice or cube. To draw out the bitter juice, line a colander with eggplant, sprinkle with salt, add another layer of eggplant, then salt, and so on. Let stand for 1 hour. Then press the eggplant against the sides of the colander before taking out and rinsing off well. Boil in fresh water for 5 minutes. Drain, reserving liquid. Pack into jars and cover with hot liquid, leaving 1-inch headspace.
Figs, fresh	Hot	Boiling-water bath	Pint Quart	45 50		Use sound, ripe fruit. Wash thoroughly. Cut large fruit in pieces. Simmer until soft; add a little water if needed. **Caution:** Add 2 tbsp. bottled lemon juice per quart or 1 tbsp. per pint to the jars; or add 1/2 tsp. citric acid per quart or 1/4 tsp. per pint to the jars. Heat to simmering and pack leaving 1/2-inch headspace.
Grapefruit	Raw	Boiling-water bath	Pint Quart	10 10		Wash and peel fruit and remove fruit segments, peeling away the white membrane, which could develop a bitter taste. Seed carefully, then pack fruit in jars and cover with boiling syrup, juice, or water, leaving 1/2-inch headspace.
Grapes	Raw	Boiling-water bath	1/2 pint Pint Quart	10 15 20		Stem, wash, and drain unripe grapes, preferably seedless. Pack tightly, but be careful not to crush. Add boiling syrup, juice, or water, leaving 1-inch headspace.
	Hot	Boiling-water bath	Pint Quart	10 10		Prepare as for raw pack, then bring fruit to a boil in syrup, juice, or water. Pack without crushing. Add boiling liquid, leaving 1-inch headspace.

Food	Style of Pack	Boiling-water Bath Canning or Pressure Canning	Jar Size	Processing Time (in Minutes)	Pressure	Procedure
Italian prunes						See Plums.
Mixed fruit	Hot	Boiling-water bath	1/2 pint Pint Quart	15 20 25		Prepare pineapples, pears, and peaches by peeling and cutting into pieces of uniform size. If you wish, add slightly underripe seedless grapes for flavor. Cook in syrup, juice, or water for 3 to 5 minutes, until slightly limp. Pack hot into jars and cover with boiling syrup, juice, or water, leaving 1/2-inch headspace.
Mushrooms	Hot	Pressure can	Pint	45	10 lbs.	Select tender, young mushrooms; discard any that have opened. Wash well, then trim off tough stalks or discolored spots. Cut in slices or leave small mushroom caps whole. Cover with water and boil for 5 minutes. Pack into hot jars, leaving 1 inch at top. Add salt (1/2 tsp. per jar) if desired. For better color, add 1/8 tsp. of ascorbic acid powder or one 500 milligram tablet of vitamin C to each pint. Add fresh, boiling water, leaving 1-inch headspace.
Nectarines	Raw or Hot	Boiling-water bath	1/2 pint Pint Quart	20 25 30		See Peaches. Use same procedure, but do not remove skins.
Okra	Hot	Pressure can	Pint Quart	25 45	10 lbs.	Choose young, tender pods only. Wash and trim ends. Leave whole or cut into 1-inch slices. Cover with hot water and boil for 2 minutes. Drain, reserving liquid. Pack into jars and cover with hot liquid, leaving 1-inch headspace.
Onions, small white	Hot	Pressure can	Pint Quart	25 30	10 lbs.	Choose onions about 1 inch in diameter. Peel, trim off roots and stalks, and wash. Cover with boiling water and cook gently for 5 minutes. Pack hot onions loosely in jar and cover with boiling liquid, leaving 1/2-inch headspace.
Oranges						See Grapefruit.
Parsnips	Raw	Pressure can	Pint Quart	20 25	10 lbs.	Wash, peel, and slice, dice, or cut into sticks. Pack to 1-1/2 inches of top, then fill with hot liquid, leaving 1-inch headspace.
	Hot	Pressure can	Pint Quart	20 25	10 lbs.	Prepare as for raw pack. Boil 3 minutes in water. Pack with hot liquid, leaving 1-inch headspace.
Peaches	Raw	Boiling-water bath	1/2 pint Pint Quart	20 25 30		Wash and remove skins by dipping fruit in boiling water for 30 to 60 seconds until skins loosen. Then dip fruit in cold water and slip off skins. Cut in half and remove pits. To prevent darkening, coat with antioxidant solution. Drain. Pack fruit in jars to 1/2 of top. Cover with boiling syrup, juice, or water, leaving 1/2-inch headspace.
	Hot	Boiling-water bath	1/2 pint Pint Quart	15 25 30		Prepare as for raw pack. Heat fruit through in hot syrup, juice, or water. Fill jars in layers, with cut side of fruit face down, and cover with cooking liquid, leaving 1/2-inch headspace.
Pears	Hot	Boiling-water bath	1/2 pint Pint Quart	15 20 25		Wash, peel, halve, and core. To prevent darkening, place in an antioxidant solution. Drain. Heat fruit through in hot syrup, juice, or water. Pack jars with hot fruit and cooking liquid, leaving 1/2-inch headspace.
Peas, green (Preferred Method: Hot)	Hot	Pressure can	Pint Quart	40 40	10 lbs.	Shell and wash. Cover with boiling water and return to a boil. Pack peas loosely in jars to 1 inch of top. Cover with cooking liquid, leaving 1-inch headspace.
	Raw	Pressure can	Pint Quart	40 40	10 lbs.	Shell and wash peas. Add salt to jars (1 tsp. per quart) if desired. Pack peas loosely in jars to 1 inch of top. Cover with boiling water, leaving 1-inch headspace.
Peas, dried						See Beans, dried.
Peppers, sweet green or red bell	Hot	Pressure can	Pint	35	10 lbs.	Remove stem, core, seeds, and inner white membrane. Remove skins by first plunging in boiling water for a few minutes, then running under cold water and taking off the split skins with a sharp knife. Add salt (1/2 tsp. per jar) and vinegar (1/2 tbsp. per jar) if desired. Slice peppers or flatten whole halves and pack carefully in layers. Cover with boiling water, leaving 1-inch headspace.
Pimientos	Hot	Pressure can	1/2 pint Pint	35 35	10 lbs.	Wash, cover with boiling water, and simmer for 4 to 5 minutes. Dunk in cold water to cool, trim stems and blossom ends, then skin them like green peppers (above). Pack flat, leaving 3/4 inch at top. **Caution:** Add 1-1/2 tsp. bottled lemon juice to each 1/2-pint jar and 1 tbsp. to each pint. Add salt (1/4 tsp. to each 1/2-pint jar; 1/2 tsp. to each pint) if desired. Cover with boiling water, leaving 1/2-inch headspace.
Pineapple	Hot	Boiling-water bath	1/2 pint Pint Quart	10 15 20		Wash thoroughly. Peel and remove eyes and core. Cut into chunks or slices of uniform size. Simmer in syrup, juice, or water for about 10 minutes. Pack and cover with syrup, juice, or water, leaving 1/2-inch headspace.
Plums	Raw	Boiling-water bath	Pint Quart	20 25		Wash. To can whole, prick skins to prevent splitting. Freestone varieties may be halved and pitted. Pack in jars to 1/2 inch of top. Cover with boiling syrup, juice, or water, leaving 1/2-inch headspace.
	Hot	Boiling-water bath	1/2 pint Pint Quart	15 25 30		Prepare as for raw pack. Heat to boiling in syrup, juice, or water. If fruit is very juicy, you may heat it with honey, adding no liquid. Pack to 1/2 inch of top. Cover with boiling syrup, juice, or water, leaving 1/2-inch headspace.

Food	Style of Pack	Boiling-water Bath Canning or Pressure Canning	Jar Size	Processing Time (in Minutes)	Pressure	Procedure
Potatoes, white, cubed	Hot	Pressure can	Pint Quart	30 35	10 lbs.	Wash, peel, and cut into 1/2-inch cubes. Dip cubes in brine (1 tsp. salt to 1 quart water) to prevent darkening. Drain. Cook for 2 minutes in boiling water. Add salt (1 tsp. per quart) to each jar. Pack hot and cover with boiling water, leaving 1-inch headspace.
Potatoes, white, whole	Hot	Pressure can	Pint Quart	30 40	10 lbs.	Wash, peel, and cook in boiling water for 10 minutes. Add salt (1 tsp. per quart) to the jars. Pack hot and cover with hot cooking liquid or boiling water, leaving 1-inch headspace.
Potatoes, sweet	Hot	Pressure can	Pint Quart	65 90	10 lbs.	Wash and sort for size. Boil or steam for 15–20 minutes, then peel. Cut into uniform pieces. Pack lightly, pressing gently, to within 1 inch of top. Cover with boiling water or syrup, leaving 1-inch headspace.
Pumpkins, cubed	Hot	Pressure can	Pint Quart	55 90	10 lbs.	Wash, halve, remove seeds, and peel. Cut into 1-inch cubes. Cover with water and boil for 2 minutes. Pack hot and cover with hot cooking liquid or boiling water, leaving 1-inch headspace.
Rhubarb	Hot	Boiling-water bath	1/2 pint Pint Quart	10 15 15		Clean; trim and discard poisonous leaves. Peel older plants (young plants do not need to be peeled). Cut stalks into 1/2-inch to 1-inch pieces. Place in large saucepan and add 1/2 cup sugar per quart of raw fruit. Let stand at room temperature for 4 hours or until juice appears. Bring slowly to a boil, then let boil for no more than 1 minute. Fill jars immediately, leaving 1/2-inch headspace.
Rutabagas						See Turnips.
Spinach (and other greens)	Hot	Pressure can	Pint Quart	70 90	10 lbs.	Pick over and wash thoroughly. Cut out tough stems and midribs. Place about 1 pound of spinach in a cheesecloth bag and steam for 3 to 5 minutes or until well wilted. Add salt (1/2 tsp. per quart) if desired. Pack loosely to 1 inch of top. Cover with boiling water, leaving 1-inch headspace.
Squash, summer						See Zucchini.
Squash, winter						See Pumpkins.
*Strawberries	Hot	Boiling-water bath	Pint Quart	10 15		Wash and hull berries. Using 3/4 cup sugar per quart of berries, spread berries one layer deep in pans and drizzle sugar over them. Cover and let stand at room temperature for 2 to 4 hours. Then place berries and juice in saucepan, and simmer for 5 minutes, stirring to prevent sticking. Pack without crushing and cover with extra boiling syrup if berries didn't produce enough juice of their own. Leave 1/2-inch headspace.
Succotash (mixed corn and beans)	Hot	Pressure can	Pint Quart	60 85	10 lbs.	Boil fresh ears for 5 minutes; cut kernels from cobs. Prepare fresh lima beans or green (snap) beans, and boil separately for 3 minutes. Measure and mix hot corn with 1/2 to an equal amount of beans. Add salt (1 tsp. per quart) if desired. Fill jars with hot mixture, leaving 1-inch headspace.
Tangerines						See Grapefruit.
Tomatoes	Hot	Boiling-water bath	Pint Quart	40 45		Wash tomatoes. Place a few at a time in boiling water just long enough to loosen skins. Then dip in cold water. Peel. Leave tomatoes whole or cut into quarters. **Caution:** Add bottled lemon juice or citric acid to jars (see page 14). Add salt (1 tsp. per quart) if desired. Bring tomatoes to a boil and pack with liquid, leaving 1/2-inch headspace. Add extra boiling water or juice if tomatoes have not made enough juice of their own.
Turnips	Hot	Pressure can	Pint Quart	30 35	10 lbs.	Wash and peel. Cube or slice. **Caution:** Do not can mashed. Cover with boiling water and boil for 3 minutes. Drain, reserving liquid. Pack into jars and cover with hot liquid, leaving 1-inch headspace.
Vegetable Mix	Hot	Pressure can	Pint Quart	60 85	10 lbs.	Use almost any mixture. Prepare each vegetable separately, then mix together and boil for 3 minutes. Pack hot and cover with boiling water, leaving 1-inch headspace.
Vegetable soups (vegetable, dried bean, meat, poultry)	Hot	Pressure can	Pint Quart	60 75	10 lbs.	Prepare according to your favorite recipe but cook only half or less than time suggested; let the soup do most of its cooking during processing. Pack and cover with boiling water, leaving 1-inch headspace. **Caution:** Process 100 minutes if soup contains seafood.
*Zucchini	Raw	Pressure can	Pint Quart	25 30	10 lbs.	Wash and slice; do not peel unless squash is large and skin is tough. Cut into 1/2-inch slices and halve or quarter slices that are extra large in diameter. Pack tightly in jars and cover with boiling water, leaving 1-inch headspace.
	Hot	Pressure can	Pint Quart	30 40	10 lbs.	Prepare as for raw pack. Cover with boiling water and bring to a boil. Drain, saving liquid. Pack loosely and cover with hot liquid, leaving 1/2-inch headspace.

acknowledgments

WE'RE DEEPLY GRATEFUL *to the many kind people who helped us create this book.*

OUR SPECIAL THANKS GO TO THE FOLLOWING:

LYNDA SPIVEY, *whose dedication, remarkable patience, unfailing tact, and incredible depth of knowledge helped us to survive—and enjoy—our research and writing*

EVAN BRACKEN (LIGHT REFLECTIONS, HENDERSONVILLE, NC), *whose photography brought our text to life in ways we never dreamed possible*

CHRIS BRYANT, *the gifted art director at Lark Books* (ASHEVILLE, NC) *whose superb design skills made this book as stunning as it is*

LAURA DOVER DORAN, *the unflappable editor at Lark Books* (ASHEVILLE, NC) *who so graciously walked us through all the difficult parts*

PATTI HILL, *without whose encouragement, humor, home-canning recipes, and kitchen, this book might never have been written*

Master food preserver **JOHN SCHNAUTZ** *and his wife,* **BARBARA** (BEARBERRY ESTATE, ASHEVILLE, NC), *whose lovely kitchen made taking our "how-to" photography a joy rather than a burden.*

JUDY CARSON *and* **TEX HARRISON.** *Tex's cookware shop,* COMPLEMENTS TO THE CHEF (ASHEVILLE, NC), *is one of the finest in the country. We know because Judy, who works there, helped us raid its inventory for our photo sessions.*

FOR HAVING CONTRIBUTED *recipes, canned foods, advice, produce, and even muscle, many thanks to*

BARBARA APPLEBAUM
master canner (FLETCHER, NC)

RALPH *and* **BETTY ASCIONE**
home canners and owners of R&B Produce
(WNC FARMERS' MARKET, ASHEVILLE, NC)

CATHERINE BALL
home canner (ASHEVILLE, NC)

JOE BRIGDON
produce clerk at Ingles grocery store (ASHEVILLE, NC)

JUDY CARSON
home canner (BARNARDSVILLE, NC)

EVANS CARTER
editorial assistant at Lark Books (ASHEVILLE, NC)

CLARA CLARK
home canner and mother of one of the authors
(HENDERSONVILLE, NC)

DAVID CRAWFORD
muscle man (HENDERSONVILLE, NC)

CAROLE CURRIE
columnist for the Asheville Citizen-Times
(ASHEVILLE, NC)

DAWN FORSBERG
home canner (SAN DIEGO, CA)

SUSIE R. GRAY
home canner (EAST POINT, KY)

PATTI HILL
master canner (WEAVERVILLE, NC)

RUTHANNE KAH
home canner (SWANNANOA, NC)

KATE MATTHEWS
home canner (BURNSVILLE, NC)

TERESA MOORE
canner for Coates Brothers Produce
(WNC FARMERS' MARKET, ASHEVILLE, NC)

EDDIE MOSES
home canner (HENDERSONVILLE, NC)

NIPPY PAGE
home canner (HENDERSONVILLE, NC)

CHARLENE ROGERS
home canner (HENDERSONVILLE, NC)

GEORGIA SHUFORD
home canner (MARION, NC)

JENNIFER THOMAS
home canner (ASHEVILLE, NC)

CINDY WHEELER
home canner (ASHEVILLE, NC)

CONNIE WHITEHEAD
home canner (STRAWBERRY PLAINS, TN)

index